ENVIRONMENTAL POLICY:

How to Apply Economic Instruments

ORGANISATION FOR ECONOMIC CO-OPERATION AND DEVELOPMENT

Pursuant to Article 1 of the Convention signed in Paris on 14th December 1960, and which came into force on 30th September 1961, the Organisation for Economic Co-operation and Development (OECD) shall promote policies designed:

— to achieve the highest sustainable economic growth and employment and a rising standard of living in Member countries, while maintaining financial stability, and thus to contribute to the development of the world economy;
— to contribute to sound economic expansion in Member as well as non-member countries in the process of economic development; and
— to contribute to the expansion of world trade on a multilateral, non-discriminatory basis in accordance with international obligations.

The original Member countries of the OECD are Austria, Belgium, Canada, Denmark, France, Germany, Greece, Iceland, Ireland, Italy, Luxembourg, the Netherlands, Norway, Portugal, Spain, Sweden, Switzerland, Turkey, the United Kingdom and the United States. The following countries became Members subsequently through accession at the dates indicated hereafter: Japan (28th April 1964), Finland (28th January 1969), Australia (7th June 1971) and New Zealand (29th May 1973). The Commission of the European Communities takes part in the work of the OECD (Article 13 of the OECD Convention).

Publié en français sous le titre :
POLITIQUE DE L'ENVIRONNEMENT :
Comment appliquer les instruments économiques

Reprinted, 1992

Foreword

The OECD has studied and called for the use of "economic instruments" in environmental protection for many years. These "Guidelines for the Application of Economic Instruments in Environmental Policy" were presented to the fourth meeting of the Environment Committee of the OECD at Ministerial level (30th-31st January, 1991) where Ministers expressed their strong support for the use of economic instruments and endorsed a Recommendation of the OECD Council on the Use of Economic Instruments in Environmental Policy which is presented in the second part of the book. The Guidelines, which are presented in the first part of the book, have been elaborated by the Secretariat, under the supervision of the Group of Economic Experts of the Environment Committee; they are published under the responsibility of the Secretary-General.

ALSO AVAILABLE

Climate Change: Evaluating the Socio-Economic Impacts (1991)
(97 90 02 1) ISBN 92-64-13462-X FF130 £16.00 US$28.00 DM50
Economic Instruments for Environmental Protection (1989)
(97 89 04 1) ISBN 92-64-13251-1 FF110 £13.50 US$23.50 DM46
State of the Environment. With supplement: Environmental Indicators. A Preliminary Set (1991)
(97 91 01 1) ISBN 92-64-13442-5 FF180 £22.00 US$38.00 DM70

Cut along dotted line

- -

ORDER FORM

Please enter my order for:

Qty.	Title	OECD Code	Price
....	....	....	....
....	....	....	....
....	....	....	....
....	....	....	....
		Total :	....

- Payment is enclosed ☐
- Charge my VISA card ☐ Number of card ....
  (Note: You will be charged the French franc price.)
  Expiration of card .... *Signature* ....
- *Send invoice. A purchase order is attached* ☐

Send publications to *(please print):*
  Name ....
  Address ....
  ....
  ....

Send this Order Form to OECD Publications Service, 2, rue André-Pascal, 75775 PARIS CEDEX 16, France, or to OECD Publications and Information Centre or Distributor in your country *(see last page of the book for addresses).*

Prices charged at the OECD Bookshop.

THE OECD CATALOGUE OF PUBLICATIONS and supplements will be sent free of charge on request addressed either to OECD Publications Service, or to the OECD Distributor in your country.

Contents

Part I

Guidelines for the Application of Economic Instruments in Environmental Policy

Chapter I

Scope and Purpose of Guidelines

1.1   Introduction

Since the creation of the Environment Committee in 1970, the OECD has regularly carried out and promoted work on the use of economic instruments in environmental policy. Following the two Recommendations of the Council on the Polluter-Pays Principle (1) in 1972 and 1974, the use and potential role of economic instruments was analyzed in a number of reports and publications (2).

Several Council Recommendations and OECD Ministerial Declarations call for the use of economic instruments for pollution control, in particular in the fields of water, waste and noise. It is generally recognized that economic instruments provide "more flexibility, efficiency and cost-effectiveness" in environmental policy (3).

OECD work on economic instruments recently culminated in a major study on the use of economic instruments in OECD Member countries (4). This study revealed that the use of economic instruments had increased significantly over the last fifteen years: in the fourteen countries reviewed (in 1987) there were over 150 instances of applications of economic instruments including systems of financial aid. Since then, several countries have reported the implementation of new economic instruments, or plans to do so.

Twenty years ago, economic instruments were used in exceptional instances only, and were subject to harsh controversy and strong resistance in every circle, namely industry, government and the general public. Nowadays, there is large consensus that, in many cases, economic instruments can be a powerful complement to direct regulations. Recent declarations at highest political level call for a wider and more consistent use of these instruments (5). The plea for a "sustainable development" path and the need to cope with transfrontier and global pollution issues requires the development of new and effective policies and economic instruments will have an important part to play.

This rapid growth in the use of economic instruments calls for the development of common guidelines or principles between Member countries with the purpose of:

--   taking stock of and drawing lessons from available experience in Member countries;

--   developing a common understanding on the nature, purpose and operation of economic instruments;

--   helping Member countries in the development and implementation of economic instruments;

--   facilitating concerted action at international level, as appropriate (see Chapter V, below).

It should be underlined that these guidelines are based on the experience gained in Member countries in applying economic instruments over the last ten to fifteen years. However, the situation is now evolving rapidly and some revision of these guidelines may be required within a few years when further experience would be obtained.

1.2   Definition and purpose of economic instruments

Economic instruments constitute one category amongst others of environmental policy instruments designed to achieve environmental goals. They can be used as a substitute or as a complement to other policy instruments such as regulations and co-operative agreements with industry. The purpose of these guidelines is not to assert a general and a priori superiority of economic instruments over other approaches but 1) to identify the circumstances and conditions under which economic instruments can provide the best results in terms of environmental effectiveness and economic efficiency and 2) to specify their modalities of implementation.

Economic instruments can be defined as instruments that affect costs and benefits of alternative actions open to economic agents, with the effect of influencing behaviour in a way that is favourable to the environment (4). They typically involve either a financial transfer between polluters and the community (e.g. various taxes and charges, financial assistance, user charges for services, product taxes), or the actual creation of new markets (for example, marketable permits).

One basic objective of economic instruments is to ensure an appropriate pricing of environmental resources in order to promote an efficient use and allocation of these resources. If the environment is priced correctly, environmental goods and services are treated equal to any other production factor in the marketplace and an economically efficient allocation of production factors is ensured. Correct pricing - in the case of pollution - implies that in the situation of an optimal use of the environment, the marginal pollution reduction costs are equal to the marginal environmental damage costs.

However, environmental goods and services are generally not marketable. Although quite a number of methods have been developed for approaching environmental prices (such as hedonic pricing, contingent valuation)(6), there is in general no proper information about the correct environmental prices (or marginal damage costs). Then, a **second-best approach** is to equalize marginal costs of environmental protection by putting a price per unit on pollution discharged. An efficient situation is thus achieved, since a given amount of pollution is reduced against minimum overall costs. Such environmental prices could be incentive environmental charges. Dependent on the circumstances, least-cost solutions can also be reached by tradeable pollution allowances. This **cost-saving potential is a major characteristic of economic instruments.**

In real world situations, however, a large gap between theory and practice often prevails. The review of past experience in OECD countries (4) shows that although charges constitute the most commonly used economic instrument, their application is largely sub-optimal. As a matter of fact, charges are usually not fixed at appropriate levels (i.e. high enough to achieve environmental goals) thus producing a lower incentive effect and/or being mainly designed for revenue-raising purposes.

All environmental charges provide financial revenue and there are several alternatives for the use of this revenue:

--   One possibility is the earmarking of funds to polluters discharging the same types of pollutants on the condition they achieve pre-determined abatement goals. In order to be perfectly consistent, such payments should be designed to fill the gap between the level of pollution abatement induced by the actual (but still too low) levels of charges and the desired level of abatement. This practice is prevailing in some countries in the field of water management.

--   A second possibility is to allocate revenue to the financing of environment related public goods or services such as collective treatment facilities, monitoring systems or administrative procedures. This is the case of **user charges**, commonly applied to waste and water management, some types of **product charges** and of **administrative charges**.

--   A third possibility is to affect charges revenue to the general government budget without specific earmarking purposes.

It should be underlined that when environmental charges do reach incentive levels (i.e. achieve environmental objectives) earmarking revenue would lead to economically inefficient solutions by inducing over investment and over expenditure in pollution control. (When charges induce polluters to abate pollution up to a desired level, there is no need to spend more resource in pollution abatement).

Marketable pollution allowances can also provide revenue if initial allowances are sold or auctioned.

Generally speaking, the revenue-raising feature of economic instruments raises the issue of revenue or budged "neutrality". On the one hand, revenues may be considered as an additional fiscal resource. On the other hand, the increased burden imposed by environmental charges may be offset by decreasing other existing taxes. This can result in tax reforms whereby some taxes are decreased while new "environmental taxes" are introduced. This approach is followed in some countries and contemplated in others.

1.3   Economic instruments and "mixed" approaches

Economic instruments are operated in isolation in few instances only. Deposit-refund systems are an example in this respect. The same may be true for user charges for the collection of household waste. There are many cases where specific economic instruments are applied in conjunction with other instruments.

Firstly, combinations of an economic instrument and direct regulation are quite common. Some economic instruments are a part of such a combination, by definition. Examples are non-compliance fees and emissions trading. Emission charges are combined with direct regulation quite generally, either to reinforce such regulation, or to provide for necessary funds.

Secondly, economic instruments may precede adjustments of existing regulations or a new regulation. Major direct regulations take time to be designed or adjusted, particularly if international bodies are involved. Temporary measures with a financial character might speed up compliance with direct regulation in advance of their actual implementation.

Thirdly, sometimes a combination of two economic instruments can be fruitful. Examples are deposit-refund systems (for instance for packaging) and a product charge on non-returnable components. The instrument of tax differentiation actually consist of a charge on a traditional product and a subsidy on the clean(er) substitute.

Nevertheless, there will always be a role for regulation: for example where flexibility of response cannot be allowed or where it is imperative that the emission of certain toxic pollutants or the use of hazardous products or substances be wholly prohibited, then governments must rely on regulators to enforce compliance. But the case in favour of regulation has been built on a broader base: proponents of regulatory approaches also call in aid the flexibility and responsiveness of regulation to different and changing circumstances. Regulation by way of standards may not always meet these requirements: standards can be rigid and inflexible. But at their best regulators can respond quickly to new events and new technologies -rules can be modified and new options considered quickly. Further, rules can be made which fit the circumstances of particular plants or localities.

In practice the information available to the regulators will be limited, and it is unlikely that they will be able to operate effectively as both pollution engineers and economists -although, this is required. The case for economic instruments is that markets are much better than individuals at processing a multiplicity of information, and that the result will be a better allocation of resources. In particular, markets are much better at establishing trade-offs between apparently different areas of activity.

Yet even where economic instruments are successfully implemented, there remains a role for regulation as the means of ensuring that the basis for market transactions is properly defined. Such regulation will probably be implemented by traditional modes -notably by government inspectors- but there are possibilities for new modes of regulation, e.g. greater use of legal remedies to enforce property rights (assuming that such rights have been properly defined).

In summary, theoretical analysis and experience gained so far in Member countries indicate that economic instruments contain a number of inherent advantages :

-- *They can yield substantial cost-savings by allowing polluters to determine the most appropriate ways of meeting a given standard (as in the case of "bubble", offset or trading systems) or by equating the marginal cost of environmental protection to the level of emissions charges across the whole range of activities.*

-- *They offer an ongoing incentive to reduce pollution below the levels determined by regulations. They also encourage new pollution control technology, production processes and new non-polluting products by favouring new research and development activities.*

-- *They increase flexibility. For the authorities, it is often easier and faster to modify and adjust a charge than to change legislation or regulation; for polluters, the freedom to choose within an overall financial constraint is preserved.*

-- *They can promote resource conservation and transmission to future generations in the same way that resource-pricing does.*

-- *They may provide a source of finance, which may either be directed to specific environmental programmes, or used as a significant instrument in overall fiscal policy.*

Chapter II

General Guidelines for the Application of Economic Instruments to Environmental Protection

2.1 Types of economic instruments to which guidelines may apply

Within the context of providing guidelines for the application of economic instruments, the following types of instruments have already been mentioned and will be dealt with in the remainder of this document. Each of these instruments has proven its practical value in one or more instances:

1)   Environmental charges or taxes

2)   Marketable permits

3)   Deposit-refund systems

Subsidies are another form of economic instruments although they can lead to economically inefficient situations. As a general rule, they are incompatible with the Polluter-Pays Principle, except when complying with the exceptions defined in the two OECD Council Recommendations on "Guiding Principles Concerning International Aspects of Environmental Policies" [C(72)128] and on "The Implementation of the Polluter-Pays Principle" [C(74)223]. However, subsidies remain a form of economic instrument which can be effective in certain circumstances, such as payments for positive externalities, cleaning up of derelict sites, catching up pollution backlog. It is also generally accepted that the revenue of pollution charges may be earmarked to achieve environmental protection goals. Therefore, references will be made to subsidies in some specific cases.

It should also be stressed that, in a number of cases, **removing** existing distorting subsidies can be an effective environmental protection measure, in particular, subsidies inducing over supply of environmental damaging goods or activities (e.g. transport or subsidizing coal mining while taxing CO_2 emissions).

Other market related instruments such as environmental liability and damage compensation schemes, performance bonds, product labelling are not covered in these guidelines, nor is the issue of natural resource-pricing.

Environmental charges: emission charges and product charges

Charges are a straightforward way to put prices on the use of the environment. In practice, they work out either as emission charges or as product charges.

Emission charges are charges on the discharge of pollutants into air, water or on the soil and on the generation of noise. Emission charges are calculated as to the quantity and quality of the pollutant. Here, the distinction between emission charges and user charges must be clearly made. In the OECD report on Economic Instruments for Environmental Protection (4), user charges have been defined as payments for the costs of collective or public treatment of effluent (including waste). **User charges** (including charges for recovery of administrative costs) have a revenue-raising purpose, by definition, and only those who are connected to the public service are charged; user charges can be directly related to the amount of pollution discharge. As to emission charges, not the public service but the act of discharging forms the basis of the charge system. Emission and user charges are widely used in OECD countries, in particular in the fields of water and waste and, to a lesser extent, in air management and noise abatement.

Product charges are charges levied on products that are harmful to the environment when used in production processes, consumed or disposed of. They can be applied to products that cause environmental problems either because of their volume or as a consequence of their toxicity or of certain harmful contents, such as heavy metals, PVC, CFC, halogenated hydrocarbons, nitrogen and phosphorus.

Product charges can act as a substitute for emission charges when directly charging emissions is not feasible for whatever reasons. Product charges may be applied to raw materials, intermediate or final (consumer) products. Economic instruments, in general, should contribute to the introduction of integrated life-cycle management. This approach is aimed at minimizing the environmental impacts of each step of the product life-cycle. The rates of product charges should reflect the environmental costs caused in each step if no other charges are applied. There is a wide range of application of product charges throughout OECD countries (charges on fuels, containers, fertilizers, pesticides, detergents etc.).

Marketable permits

Marketable permits are environmental quotas, allowances, or ceilings on pollution levels that, once initially allocated by the appropriate authority, can be traded subject to a set of prescribed rules. Their primary advantage is that they can reduce the cost of compliance; the prescribed rules are those necessary to ensure attainment of the environmental goal as trades occur. Marketable permit systems are often referred to as: emission trading programmes; tradeable permits; credit systems; or averaging. The units of exchange are referred to as credits, allowances or marketable permits. They always require an underlying set of requirements.

Marketable permits are potentially applicable in all media and economic sectors. Examples of existing systems include:

-- "Bubbles", in which two existing stationary sources of air pollution are permitted to readjust their assigned emission limits (with one source's limit being raised while the other source's limit is lowered) as long as the resulting emission limits yield equal or better environmental results.

-- "Offset" programmes under which a firm can enter or expand a polluting activity in a geographic area in which an increase in pollution levels is prohibited. Under the "offset" programme the firm wishing to increase its emissions can buy allowances from other firms already located in the area, which must then abate their emissions by the amount that is necessary to at least maintain the ambient environmental level.

-- Production quotas, in which assigned levels of production, say of CFC's can be traded among CFC producers.

Trades can be external (between different enterprises) or internal (between different plants, products, etc. of the same firm). In the latter case, no financial trading transactions take place.

Deposit-refund systems

In deposit-refund systems a deposit is paid on potentially polluting products. When pollution is avoided by returning the products or their residuals, a refund follows. This instrument has the attractive element of rewarding good environmental behaviour.

17

Deposit-refund systems are operated since long in the field of beverage containers. Their origin is purely economical: returnable bottles used to be cheaper than non-returnable bottles. Presently, private business decisions are more in favour of disposable packaging, due to the availability of cheaply produced materials. Environmental authorities see more than one reason to maintain deposit-refund systems for environmental benefits. Since substantial parts of household waste consist of packaging, deposit-refund systems can considerably reduce waste volumes. Furthermore, such systems can contribute to prevention of the release of toxic substances into the environment, for instance from disposal of batteries, incineration of plastics or residuals from pesticides containers. Deposit-refund system may be desirable as part of integrated life-cycle management for certain products for proper handling (electric appliances). There is a wide variety of applications of deposit refund systems in OECD countries, on products such as containers, batteries, car hulks.

2.2   Criteria for choice of instruments

General

When developing new policies, it should be assessed case by case whether, in which circumstances and in which form economic instruments would be most appropriate. The choice of environmental policy instruments can be made against five sets of criteria:

i)   Environmental effectiveness: Policy objectives may be to achieve certain limits on local concentrations of a given pollutant, or to achieve ambient standards defined at either a local or a wider level. Alternatively, it may be a requirement to limit total emissions of a given substance at a regional or global level. Clearly the effectiveness of given instruments must be judged against these environmental standards. The environmental effectiveness of economic instruments is mainly determined by the ability of polluters to react. Economic instruments will yield greater environmental effectiveness if they can provide a permanent incentive to pollution abatement and technical innovation. The ability of economic instruments to apply to the main target pollutants, products or substances should also be carefully assessed.

ii)   Economic efficiency: The widest definition of economic efficiency is that policy should achieve the optimal allocation of resources -- both in terms of the amount of pollution and expenditure on avoiding and accomodating pollution. But a more limited definition of efficiency is that the compliance costs associated with a given environmental benefit should be minimised. Attention should be given both to the direct costs of pollution abatement technologies and the indirect costs in terms of opportunities foregone. Policy makers should recognise that pollution control policy may have significant effects on industrial structures and technical developments, and should ideally assess costs in these terms. Economic efficiency of economic instruments will be best achieved if marginal pollution abatement costs vary significantly between polluters or when demand elasticities of polluting products and substances are high.

iii) *Equity:* Different policy instruments have different distributive consequences. Pollution charges entail additional payment on the discharge of "residual" pollution. The affectation of charge revenue result in different distributive consequences. The initial allocation of tradeable pollution allowances also implies different distributive effects. Furthermore, equity can have different meanings: for instance, equal discharge standards may imply widely unequal marginal and/or total abatement costs between polluters and pollutees.

iv) *Administrative feasibility and cost:* All types of policy instruments involve implementation and enforcement structures. This relates in particular to the ease and cost of monitoring discharges (direct monitoring or proxy variables) and the degree of coverage of main target groups.

v) *Acceptability*: It is of crucial importance that target groups accept the economic instruments imposed on them. Major resistance will render the instrument inefficient. In general, the success of any (economic) instrument requires certainty and stability over time with respect to their basic elements. Acceptability increases by taking into account the following elements:

-- **Adequate information** of target groups about any aspect of the new instrument they might be interested in. Important features are the purpose and technicalities of the instrument, financial consequences, time of introduction, possible future adjustments, etc. New elements must be timely announced. Target groups should also be aware of the interrelations between different policy fields. This is particularly important for transport policy.

-- **Consultation** with target groups which should as far as possible be involved in the execution of the instruments. Firms should be present or represented by branch organizations in the governing boards of the responsible bodies. Major modifications should be discussed with organizations representative for other, diffuse target groups (industry, farmers, consumers etc.). Instruments on the interface of different policy fields should be presented to all parties concerned.

-- **Progressive Implementation** of new economic instruments which should be preceded by an appropriate anticipation period and a timely announcement. The implementation should also be progressive, especially for emission charges and emissions trading in order to enable polluters to adapt and avoid excessively rapid increases in financial burdens (e.g. the rates of pollution charges should raise progressively up to the desired level). Furthermore, the prospect of a substantial financial burden on polluting behaviour will induce firms to take into account such burdens in their investment decision.

Criteria for choice of specific economic instruments

Emission charges should be given particular consideration for stationary pollution sources and where marginal abatement costs vary across polluters (the wider the variation, the greater the cost-saving potential). Other criteria are: the feasibility of monitoring emission (direct monitoring or proxy variables), the ability of polluters to react to the charge, the ability of public authorities to develop a consistent framework for charges, the potential for technical innovation.

Product charges should especially be applied to products that are consumed or used in large quantities and in diffuse patterns. This applicability to diffuse sources is an important feature of product charges. Products subject to charges should be readily identifiable. A special case of the product charge is the charge or tax differentiation. Product price differentials can be applied in order to discourage the consumption of polluting products and simultaneously encourage the consumption of cleaner alternatives. When a product is highly toxic and when its use should be drastically or completely reduced, partial or total ban is preferable to charges. The higher the demand elasticity and substitution possibilities of products, the higher the effectiveness of product charges.

Product charges may have one of both functions earlier mentioned in this document, i.e. for incentive purpose or for raising revenues. The level of the charge rates primarily depends on the objectives of the charge. For financing charges the charge rate is determined by the revenues required annually, the pollution unit (charge base) and the number of products sold. The rates of incentive charges depend on a number of factors, such as the price elasticity of the demand for these products, the availability of clean or cleaner substitutes and the objectives of the charge in terms of overall pollution reduction through a decline of the number of products consumed.

Product charges may have various points of impact. Firstly, they may operate as a surtax on excise duty, e.g. on mineral oil and oil products. Secondly, products with a reduced VAT tariff may be brought under the normal tariff structure. Thirdly, a surcharge could be laid on the price on products. Then, a separate calculation and invoice system must be established.

Deposit-refund systems should be considered for products or substances which can be reused, recycled or which should be returned for destruction. Such products should be easy to identify and to handle. Users and consumers should also be able and willing to take part in the scheme. The level of deposits should be monitored in relation to the level of return and not exceed the value of the material or product.

Marketable Permit Systems offer particular advantages in situation in which:

-- The marginal costs of compliance with uniform standards are non-homogeneous across the regulated target group; the greater the cost differences, the greater the potential benefits of trading;

-- Generic standards are less stringent than should be desirable for environmental reasons, due to the occurrence of excessive economic impacts on parts of the regulated target groups;

-- The environmental goal is fixed and the market can set the price (i.e., cost of compliance);

-- Greater incentives are needed to seek out improved control technology;

-- The number of sources involved is large enough to establish a well-functioning, competitive market with credits available to trade. However, in some situations even just a few large trades may justify a marketable permit programme.

Situations in which trading schemes may be constrained or not applicable include:

-- Trading schemes are not applicable to more than one pollutant simultaneously, unless some "equivalence index" exists or can be developed.

--   Trading schemes may result in negative local environmental impacts if the effect of emissions is sensitive to the location of the emissions's source especially when toxic substances are involved.

--   Problematic or expensive administrative approval requirements may be prohibitive.

In setting up specific marketable permit schemes some basic rules must be taken into account. They regard i) initial distribution (assigned baseline) of emission limits or production quotas (with respect to products) among parties under the trading scheme, ii) the way goals of the trading schemes are expressed, iii) rules on permissible trades, iv) ensurance of equivalence or improvement of environmental goals and v), in the case of products the point of impact in the production chain.

i)   Initial distribution of emission or production quotas may include:

--   direct allocation, i.e.:

--   pre-assigned baseline, i.e. assignment of initial emission limits determined by a regulatory programme;

--   "grandfathering", i.e. the determination of a baseline or initial allocation of credits/permits based on the actual or allowable emissions of an existing source at some previous time; this approach may provide permit holders with monopoly power or constrain new firms seeking to enter the market, unless these possibilities are carefully considered in the design of the trading scheme.

--   various types of auctions;

This initial distribution is important for the acceptability of the programme as the choice made has a significant effect on the distribution of the cost burden of the programme. Further, the choice will involve such issues as : should credit be given for past control actions?

ii)   Initial goals (the baseline): the initial goals (baselines) must be expressed in specific terms and be operational at the level of the individual polluter, emission point, or product to be regulated and must readily allow for the reallocation of control requirements among sources.

iii)   Rules of permissible trading could imply:

      --   unconstrained trading, which is preferable if trading rules can be clearly and comprehensively specified at the start; in this situation, trading would take place freely and directly between participants in the market with no governmental intervention.

      --   constrained trading (i.e. with detailed review and advanced approval of each individual transaction) may be necessary otherwise. In such situations, the scope of the programme or the number of anticipated transactions may have to be limited in order to ensure proper administration.

iv)   Trading schemes must ensure equivalence or improvement of the environmental goal, for instance by limiting geographic scope for trades, requiring special modelling or monitoring procedures, or imposing extra constraints on hours of operation or capacity utilization, as appropriate (i.e., not in all cases), otherwise environmental goals may be jeopardized or "windfall" credits may be created. However, establishing excessive conditions should be balanced against transaction costs and complexity.

v)   In the case of products, trading schemes may focus on a variety of points in the production chain, i.e. the point of production, at retail purchase, or at actual emission.

2.3   General guidelines

Guidelines for the application of economic instruments should directly be based on ex ante evaluation criteria. These criteria are the above-mentioned principles of environmental effectiveness, economic and administrative efficiency (related to minimisation of compliance costs and administrative costs respectively) equity and acceptability. For practical purposes, i.e. proposing guidelines for design, introduction and enforcement of economic instruments, these criteria should be elaborated into a set of checkpoints, which are listed below:

Clear framework and objectives

First and foremost, framework and objectives of the economic instrument under study must be clear. Does the economic instrument operate in combination with direct regulation? Or does it precede regulations in order to speed up compliance? Or will the economic instrument serve as an alternative or as a substitute to direct regulation? Or is there a financial purpose only (charges)? Are the revenues used for general purposes or are they earmarked for specific environmental measures? In the case of charges, the formally stated goal (to provide incentives) should not be confused with the revenue-raising purpose.

Well-defined field of operation

The field of operation must be clearly defined. This includes pollutants, processes or products under the regime of the economic instruments. Furthermore, information should be available on the target groups in terms of their number, their size, their contribution to the pertinent problem, their location and the way they pollute (point/non-point sources, mobile/stationary sources), their financial abilities and the way they are organised. However, information requirements should not be too heavy (see also below). Target groups should be carefully identified and characterised according to the environmental field and economic sectors which are concerned (see Sections 3 and 4).

Simple mode of operation

Simplicity and clarity of the mode of operation are of paramount importance and determine to a large extent the administrative efficiency of the economic instrument. This is related to the technicalities of the economic instrument: formulae for the charge base, the way of calculation of the charge, calculation of emission reduction credits, etc. Furthermore, it regards the administrative requirements in terms of new bodies (or association with existing tax offices), the way monitoring will take place and the details of the invoice and control. Regarding the "structure" of any economic instrument there should be a fine balance between undue complexity, which makes the instrument hard to apply, and excessive simplicity, which may mean that it is not very efficient. It should be stressed that the amount of information required for proper operation of any instrument is of decisive importance for its success. Economic instruments aiming at affecting behaviour of polluters are likely to be more complex than those designed for purely revenue-raising purpose. The simplicity or complexity of the mode of operation is mainly related to the calculation and invoicing procedures:

For **emission charges**, three ways of calculating the bill exist: 1) by monitoring actual discharges, 2) table-based, 3) a flat rate. Actual monitoring might be done either by the responsible administrative body in a yearly or more frequent sequence, or by the polluter himself through yearly (or more frequent) returns. Self-monitoring is less costly, but requires a periodic control. Actual monitoring is recommendable for large polluters. A table-based charge calculation is established through a single operation, taking into account general indicators such as certain process characteristics, the number of employees of the firm, etc. The closer the link between polluting emissions and the payment, the more effective the charge is.

Product charge rates are fixed. Recalculation should take place if the charge lacks incentive or financial power.

For **marketable permits**, constant or decreasing emission ceilings must be defined. Furthermore, it should be decided whether a net reduction of total discharges must be achieved, and to what extent. Provisions must be made with respect to new entrants in the market.

Regarding **deposit-refund systems**, the refunds should be high enough to encourage return, but not so high as to discourage production.

Regarding **invoicing**, any system that fits in with existing financial channels has clear administrative advantages. For product charges, taxing systems (excise duties, value-added tax) are efficient structures. Invoicing many different product charges at the retailers' level should be avoided. Producers and importers are less in number, and therefore more efficiently administrated and more easily controlled.

Integration with Sectoral Policies

Economic instruments should be designed to facilitate the integration of environmental policy with other policies, in particular through an appropriate adaptation of various economic sectors' pricing and fiscal structures to environmental goals. Removal and correction of governmental intervention failures such as distorting subsidies in the agricultural field or improper pricing of transport infrastructures, fuels and services, are of utmost importance for a proper integration of environmental policies with sectoral policies. One fundamental objective of economic instruments is to ensure that the price of goods and services truly reflects the associated environmental cost. This can be achieved only if intervention failures are first removed.

Manpower and cost of implementation

Any new instrument requires manpower and financial means for implementation and enforcement. Careful assessment is necessary. Particularly for financing charges and tradeable emission rights, excessive collection and transaction costs should be avoided. The cost effectiveness of implementation and enforcement mechanisms should be carefully assessed. Using existing enforcement channels and invoicing systems could provide substantial cost savings.

Assessment of economic and distributive consequences

The (economic) significance of the instruments determines on the one hand the results in terms of reduced pollution or financial revenues, and on the other hand the financial consequences for target groups, possible hardship and the need for temporary aid, and possible evasion. The administrative structure also determines the costs of execution, which might be prohibitive when compared to the results that are aimed for.

In dealing with the economic consequences of economic instruments, a clear distinction should be drawn between the economic impact linked to the level of environmental objectives as such (e.g. ambient quality levels) and the specific consequences of applying economic instruments rather than, or in addition to, regulations. Several aspects should be distinguished. Firstly, at micro level, specific (groups of) enterprises may have to face considerable expenditures in a short period of time, which may threaten their continuity. On the other hand, at a more macro level, the instrument concerned will establish efficient solutions in the longer term, if defined according to correct principles. In comparing general long term efficiency and specific short term problems, temporary financial measures for easing such problems should be preferred, provided that the firms concerned basically have a healthy economic structure, even when increased environmental costs are accounted for. Applying temporary measures is economically more justifiable than granting exemptions of the imposed instrument. Economic instruments, however, have positive economic consequences; for instance, emission tradings have allowed for ongoing economic growth which would not have been possible under strict direct regulation. Incentive charges (but also direct regulation) may trigger technological innovations, which may create new markets and even provide new export products.

A second aspect is the occurrence of undesirable changes in the income distribution. The application of economic instrument may seriously affect low-income groups. Although such effects may be part of an efficient solution, exemptions or other measures may be considered for reasons of equity.

Conformity with general principles of national and international trade, fiscal and environmental policy

Both at the national and at the international level general principles of environmental policy have been agreed on. One of the most important is the "Polluter-Pays" Principle. Economic instruments, with the exclusion of financial assistance, clearly are in line with this principle. Other principles that must be respected stem from trade agreements (GATT). When introducing economic instruments, unfair competition and international trade distortion must be avoided. International trade is an important factor in reaching optimal efficiency on an international scale, since comparative cost advantages of the trade partners are fully exploited. Therefore, GATT-rules state that no differential tax burdens should be imposed which would create undue trade distortion. In particular, charges should not discriminate between domestic and imported products. These rules, however, are based on the traditional theory of international trade and ignore environmental damage costs, implying that optimal efficiency on the national scale already exists. When greater efficiency is sought, the application of environmental charges is desirable and differences in charge rates, due to differences in national conditions, are quite conceivable (See Chapter V).

Economic instruments should be in concordance with the existing political, administrative, judicial and fiscal structures. On the international level, economic instruments should be compatible with agreements such as the Basel Convention and the Montreal Protocol. If economic instruments do not fit into existing frameworks or require their modification, the actual implementation will be made considerably complex and difficult. Since in many instances economic instruments have a fiscal character, their compatibility with existing fiscal systems is particularly important. The application of economic instruments can be greatly facilitated if existing financial and tax channels can be used.

Chapter III

Guidelines for the Application of
Economic Instruments to Environmental Sectors

3.1   Water pollution

i)   *Background*

    This Section is restricted to inland water systems, including ground water. Water quality policy is one of the few environmental policy field where economic instruments have traditionally played a relatively strong role.   Charges for the collection and treatment of waste water are well established in most Member countries (user charges).   In fewer instances, charges are also applied to polluters who discharge their effluent directly into open water (emission charges). Combinations of direct regulation and economic instruments (notably charges) have gained results, particularly in the field of oxygen-demanding substances. It is felt however that the pollution burdens of rivers are still too high and even increasing in some cases. Common problems for many countries are nutrients, heavy metals and other toxic substances. Economic instruments should reinforce direct regulations and add new incentives for changing polluters behaviour. Possibilities of applying economic instruments vary according to the type of source, namely point sources and non-point sources. Instruments which require direct monitoring are only applicable to point sources.

ii)   *Purpose and framework*

    The purpose of water pollution charges is either to finance necessary (collective) measures for waste water collection and purification, or to provide financial incentives for a reduction of the discharges of effluent. These purposes will not coincide in general, unless some complementarity is realised: charge rates induce pollution abatement up to a certain, albeit insufficient, level and further abatement is achieved through payments paid out of charge-revenue.

Economic instruments for water quality policy mainly act in the context of direct regulations. In some instances, an isolated application of economic instruments is conceivable. In the case of diffuse pollution by many polluters, for example, direct regulation is hardly applicable. An example is the reduction of nutrient run-off from agricultural land. Then, particularly product charges can be envisaged.

iii) *Types of economic instruments*

Emission (effluent) charges

Each of the economic instruments discerned in Chapter 2 is applicable in the field of water quality policy. Emission (effluent) charges are a traditional type, applied since long in some countries. Emission charges can be based either on the quality and quantity of waste water or, as a proxy, on water polluting processes.

Product charges

Product charges are conceivable in the case of products that will pollute surface or ground water before, during or after consumption. Examples are detergents, fertilizers and pesticides. If the objective of the product charge is to discourage consumption, the products concerned should have a not too small price elasticity. The availability of cleaner substitutes could considerably increase the success of product charges or differentiated charges (such as detergents with and without phosphates). Product charges can also be used as a proxy for emission charges (e.g. charge on the use of polluting products in production processes).

Marketable permits

Marketable permits are applicable to point sources as well as to combinations of point sources and non-point sources. Authorities define a total level of the pertinent pollutant and sell or grant emission rights to all actors involved. In the case of point sources firms can gain additional rights by purchasing them or by reducing their pollution. In the case of point source/non-point source situations, point sources could obtain additional rights by reducing the pollution burden from non-point sources, for example by financing best available agricultural practices.

Deposit-refund systems

Finally, deposit-refund systems can play a role in this policy field. Many potentially polluting substances (for example, pesticides) are packed in non-returnable containers. During disposal the remnants of these substances are released into the environment and might pollute surface and ground water. Such remnants can properly be processed, when containers are returned to the producer.

iv)   *Field of operation*

Pollutants/processes/products

Next to oxidizable matter (OM), suspended solids, nutrients (P, N), organic chlorine compounds, salt (Cl), heavy metals (CD, Hg, Pb, As, etc.) and toxic substances (halogenated (hydro)carbons) are the main water pollutants. Pollutants which are discharged in large quantities by many dischargers and which are easy to calculate or monitor or for which a common denominator that allows for trade-offs exists (BOD, COD) can more easily be subjected to emission charges than pollutants that occur in great variety and small amounts (heavy metals, toxic substances). For the latter, product charges are more conceivable. Because of the complexity of the matter a multi-phase approach is necessary, starting with those pollutants that are easiest to handle and lead to substantial results.

v)   *Mode of operation: formulae and implementation*

Formulae

In designing economic instruments a controversy between efficiency and effectiveness may exist. Regarding emission charges, a detailed charge base addressing all relevant pollutants and fine-tuned charge rates is effective (and desirable from a theoretical point of view), but such a system is not efficient due to administrative complexity and difficult enforcement. For any particular case, a balance must be sought. If applied for financing collective treatment measures, administration costs should be kept as low as possible.

Regarding product charges, too many product charges are impractical, especially when they are applied for revenue-raising. If applied, product charges act as proxies for the water pollution that products will cause before, during or after consumption. The charge base should contain those elements or byproducts that actually will affect water quality.

The level of the charge rates primarily depends on the objectives of the charge; For financing charges the charge rate is determined by the revenues required annually (for instance, based on the implementation plans of Water Boards), the pollution unit (charge base) and the total amount of pollution. A careful planning of collectively financed water treatment works is necessary, since capital costs of such installations are a large share of total costs, making total costs relatively independent from total pollution that is treated. Then, declining pollution quantity means an increasing charge rate. The rates of incentive charges should be based on a number of factors, such as the availability of clean or clean-up technology, the marginal pollution abatement costs and the objectives of the charge in terms of overall pollution reduction.

Competence

In many countries water quality policy is a regional or provincial competence, based upon administrative structures, already operational for quantitative water problems (Water Boards, River Basin Agencies). New administrative tasks following from the application of economic instruments should be executed within those bodies. If no such bodies exist, administrative regions following (river)basin boundaries could usefully be established. Water Boards are well suited to govern emission charges. Marketable permit programmes may either be governed by national, or by regional authorities, dependent on the existing direct regulation they are added on, or the scale they are applied.

Calculation

For calculation, the guidelines defined in Section 2.3 should be applicable.

Invoice

As a general rule, invoicing should ensure that charges are clearly perceived by payers as "paying for pollution". Emission charges should be invoiced either through existing Water Board financial circuits (polder tax) or together with the water bill (see also guidelines defined in Section 2.3).

vii)   **International aspects**

Water quality policy has a strong international dimension. Rivers carry pollution over long distances and many countries have a common interest in adjacent seas. International policy-making takes place e.g. in North Sea Conferences and International Rhine Conferences. As far as international dimensions are concerned, the goal of environmental policy and the design and implementation of economic instruments require concerted action, at least. Regarding charges time schedules, the modes and fields of operation should be coordinated. Due to differences in national endowments and consumer preferences and incomes, charge rates are not necessarily equal. Without international negotiations, however, average charge rates will tend to be too low, since only domestic pollution damage will be taken into account. In the case of rivers, downstream countries sometimes are inclined to partly finance solutions upstream. This policy may be economically efficient and should be governed by commonly agreed principles.

In sofar as water pollution problems are exclusively domestic, it is up to individual Member countries to define instruments they feel appropriate.

3.2   Atmospheric emissions

i)   *Background*

Air pollution occurs on many scales: on the global scale greenhouse effects and the destruction of the ozone-layer are a relatively new and serious problem. Many countries are convinced of the necessity of concerted action. On the continental scale acidification is a transfrontier as well as a national problem, still causing considerable damage to the environment. On the regional and local scale, various air pollutants and photochemical smog create problems for which definite solution are as yet not available. On the residential scale, indoor pollution receives increasing attention.

Air quality policy is a policy field where, traditionally, direct regulation has been the primary instrument. Economic instruments have had a limited application so far, with the exception of some redistributive charging systems and a number of marketable permit programmes in the United States. Among those actually implemented are: the Emissions Trading Programme (which includes bubbles, offsets netting and banking); the lead-in-gasoline phase down programme, the marketable permit programme for CFC producers (which now includes a fee component); and averaging for lines of heavy duty engines and can-coaters. Furthermore, many countries have long applied various forms of fuel charges, although primarily for financial purposes. However, introducing more extensive economic instruments has recently been considered, in particular for energy-related air pollution and for consumer products. Air quality policy has (or should have) strong integrative aspects, especially with energy and traffic policy. Economic instruments should contribute to further integration, should reinforce direct regulation and should add new powerful incentives.

ii)   *Purpose and framework*

Generally, economic instruments could function as adjuncts to direct regulation. The rationale for economic instruments is that they help save costs, may be more effective and work permanently in the direction of improved technology. Since existing fuel charges have mainly a financial goal, new charges should be clearly defined as to their purpose, be it financial or incentive. Since there is no possibility for air pollution to be abated through collective (i.e., public) measures, much attention must be given to the way the revenues of emissions charges will be allocated. Possibilities are a reduction of the product taxes or of direct taxes.

Close relations between environmental policy on the one hand, and transport and energy policy on the other hand, requires integration of new instruments of environmental policy into the other policy fields and vice versa (see also Sections 4.1 and 4.2).

iii)   *Types of economic instruments*

Emission charges

In the field of air pollution control, emission charges are quite feasible for reinforcing direct regulation and promote technical innovation. For administrative reasons (in particular, monitoring of emissions), emission charges are more easily applicable to pollutants emitted in large quantities and large stationary sources.

Product charges

Products charges have two main fields of applications. Firstly, they may be applied to products that contain air polluting substances which are released during consumption (CFC's, solvents). Secondly, product charges have a role to play regarding energy pricing. Charges on fuel in the form of a surcharge on or a variation of the excise duties on fossil fuel and products are already common. Their charge base should differ according to the purpose of the charge, be it financing or incentive. Product charges could be used as a proxy for emission charges, for instance when pollution is diffuse, when there are many, small (mobile) or area (household or small business) sources and when the product charge can serve as a proxy for the emissions charge. Especially in the traffic sector, there is a strong tradition for taxation of mobile sources, which should be reconsidered from an environmental point of view (see Section 4.1).

Creating price differentiation between traditional products and cleaner substitutes could be done by a combination of surcharges and discounts on the price of such products in a revenue-neutral way. This can have favourable effects since, in many cases, substitution-elasticities are lower than price-elasticities.

Marketable permits

In air quality policy regarding large and small industries alike, direct regulation implies technological requirements which can be extremely complex. Then, the information load for authorities can be heavy, resulting in delay and the development of regulations that are non-optimal, that is regulations which impose costs above and beyond those necessary to meet the specified environmental goal. Since trading schemes provide an opportunity for firms to meet initial regulatory requirements in alternative, and hence presumably lower cost ways, they may remove some of the pressure upon authorities to develop an initially optimal regulatory structure. Marketable permits should be considered in order to create market alternatives to mandatory requirements for existing, new and modified installations.

Marketable permits can also be studied regarding air pollution characteristics of products (e.g. cars, products containing VOC's). Producers could be allowed to trade credits they earn by doing better or earlier than required, providing that equal or better environmental results are achieved after trading.

In designing and implementing trading schemes a number of ground rules must be acknowledged. These were dealt with in Section 2.2

Deposit-refund systems

A number of products contain potentially air polluting substances (for instance, in closed circuits) which will be released in case of inappropriate disposal. Examples are refrigerators, air- conditioners and fire extinguish devices (CFC's, halons etc.). Controlled scrapping and disposal can prevent the release of these substances. Deposit-refund systems applied to products can encourage proper collection.

Other instruments

At the interface of environmental and transport policy, two economic instruments should be further considered: road pricing and "variabilisation" of the costs of car use. Road pricing is presented as a solution for rush-hour congestion which will also lead to air pollution reduction, (see Section 4.1, below).

"Variabilisation" of car costs is a special form of tax differentiation. Increasing running costs of car use, e.g. by higher excise duties on fuels, can improve the car user's perception of his real costs and hence discourage car use.

iv)   *Field of operation*

Pollutants/processes/products

Pollutants that are emitted in large quantities are carbon dioxide, sulphur dioxide, nitrogen oxides, carbon monoxide, volatile organic compounds and particulates.   Other relevant substances that occur in smaller amounts are halogenated hydrocarbons, chlorides, heavy metals and a large variety of other pollutants. Economic instruments should be applied in a progressive manner, starting with pollutants discharged in large quantities, that are easiest to handle, for which fast results can be expected, and to new emerging issues where innovative efficient policies are needed.

Emission charges should be applied to pollutants which are easy to calculate or monitor. Diffuse pollution from diverse sources could be effectively combatted by charging associated products or by applying a charge or tax differentiation in favour of products generated by cleaner technology.

Marketable permits are easily applicable to single pollutants. They may also work with respect to pollutants for which a common denominator (such as "acidification equivalents") exists. Marketable permits may be more difficult to apply or may need special constraints for substances that may have harmful effects on a very localized scale.

Regarding products, marketable permits may be used to provide cost savings, flexibility, and in some cases greater effectiveness with regulation of products characteristics, such as abolition of harmful contents, a lower energy use, etc.

A trading scheme for emissions may be easiest to apply or have broadest application when:

--   The environmental impact is independent of the source's location (e.g. CFC's) or only very loosely related (e.g. SO_x's contribution to acid rain). The more dependent the environmental impact is on the source's precise location, the more constrained the trading programme will have to be.

--   The impact of the emissions is not closely connected to the precise time of their release into the environment (i.e., the environmental impact depends on cumulative emissions over a long period of time, rather than on the quantity of emissions released over brief periods such as one hour or one day). Trading schemes can, however, be used even when impacts over short time periods are of concern.

v)   ***Mode of Operation: Formulae and Implementation***

Formulae

For **emission charges,** various pollutants should be brought together in sofar as a common denominator is available (e.g. acidifying substances). If a specific sector comprise large and small sources, a threshold should be chosen above which emissions are monitored, for reasons of administrative simplicity. Smaller sources then could pay a flat-rate or table-based charge. If smaller sources are exempted from the charge for administrative reasons, the charge revenues should be returned to the charge payers in an environmentally-neutral way.

Emission charges are the most direct, and therefore fairest way of pricing the environment. However, if a fixed link exists between the emission level (output) and some input into the process, a product charge on that output acts as a good proxy. A major example is the emission of carbon dioxide from the combustion of fuels. If, for whatever reason, it has been decided to apply a product charge aimed at reducing the emission of some pollutants that has no fixed link with the charge, a correction of the charge bill might be considered if the payer has installed emission-reducing equipment.

Product charges should be based on air pollution such products generate. For energy, the charge base should differ according to the types of fuels and the way these fuels are burned.

The effectiveness of incentive product charges depends largely on the price-elasticity of the demand for the products concerned. If cleaner substitutes exist, small price differentials might already be effective. This is important for the promotion of clean consumer products, such as clean cars, low-pollution space heating equipment, spray cans without CFC's, etc.

If **deposit-refund systems** are applied for products containing harmful substances in closed circuits, refund should be high enough to encourage return. For long-live products (refrigerators containing CFC's) the refund could be higher than the deposit, further increasing the attractiveness of return. This price difference would reflect interest received on deposited revenues.

Competence

Establishing **product charges and deposit-refund systems** could be the responsibility of national or regional authorities. For reasons of competition, agreements on international application may be recommendable. This regards energy in particular (see Section 4.2). Establishing emission charges is related to direct regulation, such as granting licenses. The broad structure of **emission charges** (charge base, etc.) could be developed at the national (or international) level. Further specification and implementation could be done by national or regional authorities, or, in general, at the level where licenses are granted.

Marketable permit programmes may either be governed by national, or by regional authorities, dependent on the existing direct regulation they are added on, or the scale they are applied. The less authorities intervene in the day-to-day operation of the market (unconstrained trading), the more efficient trading schemes will be. Authorities should strive for promulgating rules that could prevent case-by-case approvals.

Calculation and invoice

The guidelines defined in Section 2.3 should be applicable.

vi)   *International aspects*

The international dimensions of air pollution have already been mentioned in Paragraph 1. Global issues especially require a co-ordinated approach to avoid the "free rider" problem (see Chapter 5).

The integration of the European Market is an important political process which might have its repercussions for the introduction of new instruments. As a consequence of removing border controls, a process of fiscal harmonization is underway. Excise duties on mineral oil and value-added tax are important vehicles for the creation or extension of economic instruments. In this respect, an integration of European and environmental policy is necessary.

Economic instruments addressing transboundary and global air pollution must take full account of international principles and agreements. Examples are the Large Combustion Plant Directive (EC) and the Montreal Protocol for Protecting the Ozone-Layer.

Political and economic developments in East-Europe will probably result in (a better) co-ordination regarding environmental policy between East and West-Europe. For air pollution control, new economic instruments such as marketable permits for certain air pollutants with a regional impact may be conceivable on a European scale.

3.3   Waste management

i)   Background

The generation of waste is increasingly a public health problem, due to both waste volumes and toxic elements in the waste streams. To reduce both problems, it is of particular importance that products have a longer life, are reused or offered for secondary use and that dispersion of obsolete products with dangerous substances in the environment is prevented. This requires specific collection for which deposit-refund systems seems to be particularly prone. In waste management policy, economic instruments are not extensively used in general, although prices prove to be an important element in proper waste handling. One reason is that, in general, waste is easy to dispose of illegally. Another reason is that waste management is an intricate field containing many pitfalls. One of the central problems from an environmental point of view is the often unknown synergistic effects of final waste due to many different substances in a specific waste stream. The analytics of what contribution each substance makes are still poorly developed.

ii)   Purpose and framework

The purpose of applying economic instruments in waste management is either financing or incentive. Financing charges (user charges) are aimed at a proper collection, processing and storage of waste or at restoration of old hazardous waste sites. Collective processing and storage of chemical waste should be given due consideration.

Incentive charges can have multiple purposes which should be recognized when such charges are designed. A first purpose might be to minimize (voluminous and/or toxic) waste generation in production and consumption processes. A second purpose might be to discourage production and consumption of (voluminous and/or toxic) waste-intensive products and to promote more "friendly" substitutes. Thirdly, economic instruments can be introduced to promote recycling which saves depletable resources, including space for waste dumping.

In defining economic instruments for waste management, two considerations should always be taken into account: 1) any policy that implies a (higher) pricing of waste disposal induces illegal waste dumping, 2) as a consequence of the complexity of waste generation, any solution for one problem may cause a new problem elsewhere. In some cases, waste emerges from solutions to other environmental problems (e.g. removal of SO_2 from flue gases causes gypsum), whereas a waste management solution may in itself cause a new problem (e.g. injection of manure into the soil contaminates groundwater with nitrates). Taking into account the whole integrated life-cycle of raw materials, products and waste is a sine qua non condition for a proper definition of economic instruments. This is also necessary in order to avoid double, treble or even quadruple charging (raw materials, production, consumption, disposal).

iii)   Types of Economic Instruments

Generally, emission and user charges, product charges and in particular deposit-refund systems are applicable in the field of waste management. In some instances, tradeable emission rights are also conceivable.

Emission (disposal) charges

Emission (disposal) charges should be based either on the volume or on the toxicity (or other harmful characteristics) of waste elements. In the latter case, waste containing many substances will cause calculation and monitoring problems. Emission charges can only be applied if dischargers are easily controllable, because of possible evasion. In most cases, **user charges**, i.e. payment for waste collection and the use of waste disposal facilities, should be applied. Regarding household waste, a better linkage between the charge bill and the waste volume offered for collection is envisageable by charging per bag. Such a charge will appear as a product charge on waste bags.

Product charges

Product charges are conceivable in the case of products that will generate waste in the production or consumption phases. They act as proxies in those cases where a direct charging of waste is not effective or efficient. Materials which can be recycled or re-used could be charged in order to induce such course of action. Product charges on non-returning packaging can support deposit-refund systems on returnable alternatives.

Deposit-refund systems

In the cases where a return of used products to collection or storage sites is very important, a deposit-refund system could be considered. This is desirable when such products can be easily re-used or recycled (bottles, crates) or when such products contain potentially polluting substances (batteries, cars).

Products subject to deposit-refund systems should be large in quantity and a collection system should be easy to create. Stardandization will enlarge the possibilities of deposit-refund systems and will, if internationally agreed on, prevent trading problems.

Marketable permits

In certain situations, "marketable waste disposal" permits could be conceived, e.g. systems whereby manufacturers are assigned specific percentages of waste recycling and/or safe disposal could trade such permits with other manufacturers. Such schemes should, however, be complemented by prohibition to ship waste outside the regulated area; this would entail monitoring and enforcement problems. Fixing a ceiling on waste discharge is also complicated because of the composite nature of waste streams, the way they are disposed of and hence the uncertainties related to environmental impacts.

iv)   *Field of operation*

Pollutants/processes/products

"Waste" is a complex and diffuse threat to the environment and can consist of many diverse substances. From the point of view of economic instruments, several categories should be discerned: 1) used or obsolete products that can be re-used or recycled, 2) voluminous streams of residuals from large-scale production processes: industrial waste, 3) large streams of residuals from many small sources:

household waste, agricultural waste, mining waste 4) small streams of toxic waste: industrial waste. A main distinction for all categories is that between intermediate waste, still to be processed, and final waste to be disposed of.

v)   *Mode of operation: formulae and implementation*

Formulae

Regarding **emission (disposal) charges**, a detailed charge base addressing all relevant pollutants and fine-tuned charge rates, including the costs of waste handling and remaining damage, is generally not feasible in the field of waste management, because of the often unknown, composite character of many waste streams. Emission charges should be restricted to smaller numbers of larger sources with relatively hazardous waste streams of a simple composition.

Product charges act as proxies for the waste products cause, either when produced or disposed of after consumption. The charge base should contain those elements which actually cause the waste problem. This can be a problem of volume caused by large numbers of (daily) products (packaging) or a problem of toxicity caused by products with a longer life-cycle (e.g. batteries).

If **deposit-refund systems** are considered for products that can be re-used, such products should be easy to standardize (packaging, (car)batteries, car tyres). Deposit-refund systems for products and appliances that contain harmful parts are furthered by standardizing and labelling those parts.

Competence

Waste processors are partly public bodies, partly private firms. For reasons of equity and efficiency, they should be subject to the same rules and instruments. Proper waste handling is mainly a task for regional and local authorities, or special boards. They should be free to tune emission charges to the problems specific to their regions, although national authorities should be involved in definition of broad structures (charge base) and properly coordinate the use of charges in order to avoid "waste tourism" across regions.

Calculation

The charge rate of emission (disposal) charges should include two elements: 1) payment for proper collecting, processing and storage of waste including occupation of space, 2) payment for remaining damage to the environment, be it pollution of water, air, soil or for land use. Furthermore, authorities should decide on appropriate prices for the use of the environment (land fill, residual pollution), which should be valid for both public and private waste processors.

Charge rates for waste with a low toxicity generated by small sources should be table-based or flat. Total revenues should cover all relevant costs, including the price for environmental use (see also guidelines defined in Section 2.2).

Invoice

Emission charges should be invoiced at the waste sites, which are relatively few in number; they pass on the charges to their customers. Charge bills for household waste can be handled through local tax offices (see also guidelines defined in Section 2.2).

vi) *International aspects*

Waste can be shipped across borders with relative ease. This is especially so for the European Communities after the integration of the European Market and the removal of border controls. Therefore, rules for waste management should be coordinated and related tariffs should not differ considerably in order to avoid "waste tourism". This should be realized by harmonizing time schedules for the implementation of economic instruments and their modes and fields of operation.

In this respect an integration of environmental and trade policy is necessary including the notion that waste be different from normal free-tradeable products.

3.4 Noise

i) *Background*

Noise is one of the most widespread forms of pollution in industrialized countries. It is a significant public health and welfare issue. Major sources are traffic, aircraft and neighbourhood noise, though industrial and construction noise can also seriously affect liveability in residential areas. Without proper measures, noise problems are likely to increase rapidly due to economic growth and related increase of traffic and industrial activities and the lack of appropriate policy. Furthermore, road transport is likely to increase in Europe as a consequence of the market integration. Economic instruments are scarcely applied in the field of noise abatement, except for aircraft, although they should be able to play a much stronger role, especially in this policy area.

ii) *Purpose and framework*

Policy development regarding noise is proceeding too slow and enforcement is generally poor. Economic instruments should reinforce direct regulation, improve enforcement of existing measures and speed up compliance with more stringent noise standards. Economic instruments should also improve the integration between different policy fields, in particular between transport policy and noise abatement policy. Economic instruments (charges) are also able to raise revenues for financing physical measures, i.e., insulation, measures against noise transmission (noise barriers), etc.

iii) *Types of economic instruments*

The main economic instruments applicable in noise policy are emission charges and product charges.

Emission charges

Charges on noise sources should be considered regarding aircraft noise, road traffic noise and industrial noise sources. Aircraft noise charges should be applied on landing fees according to noise characteristics of the aircraft and associated with physical regulations (ICAO noise approval certificates). Charges could also be applied to passenger cars and lorries, based on their acoustic characteristics as measured under ISO procedures. Emission charges could also be applied to (stationary) industrial noise sources.

Product charges

Product charges could be used with respect to appliances. Differentiation of charges or taxes is conceivable regarding noisy products and low-noise-alternatives.

Other instruments

Economic instruments which are considered with respect to other traffic problems, such as road pricing and "variabilisation" of the costs of car use, could also work in relation to noise (see Section 4.1). Actually, noise charges could be part of an integrated charging system on motor-vehicles, comprising pollution and other possible characteristics of vehicles. Marketable permits related to noise characteristics of products (cars, tools, etc.) might be conceivable.

iv)   *Field of operation*

Pollutants/processes/products

Noise is a complicated phenomenon and appears in many patterns. Each single pattern may have various impacts on human well-being, since noise perception depends on many factors such as time of the day, background noise and other, personal, conditions. Measurement indicators are mainly based on continuous equivalent noise levels (Leq), measured in dB(A). Neighbourhood noise levels from road traffic or industrial sources are commonly measured at the facades of buildings, over 18 or 24 hours. Exposures over 65 dB(A) are considered to be serious and are the main reference for policy measures. Exposure to noise levels between 55 and 65 dB(A) is valued uncomfortable but may be serious as well under many circumstances. For aircraft noise, complicated formulae, including penal factors for night time flights, have been drawn.

In addition to transportation modes, a variety of industrial and other processes as well as industrial and household appliances give rise to noise problems.

v)   *Mode of operation: formulae and implementation*

Formulae

Preferably, noise charges could be based on indices measuring the impact of noise. Such indices could be based on the fact that the level of annoyance doubles for each 10 dB(A) increase and that a constant relationship can be established between noise levels and the percentage of people highly annoyed.

Regarding transport noise, charges should be based on noise emission levels of vehicles (aircraft, automobiles, lorries, motorcycles, etc.) as measured under international standard procedures (ISO for motor-vehicles; ICAO for aircraft). For mobile sources a link could be made to use of the vehicle, for example by charging fuels, according to their types (for instance, diesel powered engines are noisier)..

For noise emissions by industrial installations, noise levels measured in dB(A) should be used. If a specific sector comprise large and small sources, a threshold should be chosen above which emissions are monitored, for reasons of administrative simplicity. Smaller sources then should pay a flat-rate or table-based charge.

Product charges should be based on once-established noise characteristics, measured in dB(A). Standards above which product charges should be applied may vary according to the way products are used (indoor, outdoor; day or night).

Competence

Aircraft noise problems have a strong international dimension. The greater the number of airports applying aircraft noise charges, the more efficient would be the schemes. Airport authorities should be made responsible for the enforcement of charging schemes. Charges on motor-vehicles could be fixed at national level. Product charges could be a national competence too.

For industrial noise problems, national authorities could design charging schemes to be implemented by local or regional authorities, since such problems are local by definition.

Calculation and Invoice

Aircraft charges could be invoiced together with existing landing fees (see also guidelines defined in Section 2.3).

vi)   **International aspects**

The integration of the European Market is likely to push transboundary transport. Economic instruments applied to noise problems from such transport (aircraft, lorries) should be harmonized.

Noise standards applied to noise characteristics of internationally traded products (cars, appliances) should be harmonized in order to avoid trade distortion.

Chapter IV

Applying Economic Instruments to Key Economic Sectors

In implementing economic instruments, careful consideration must be given to the characteristics of the economic agents and sectors to which they may apply. Different economic sectors may be more or less prone to the use of economic instruments due to the specificity of the environmental issues, the structure of the sector, the type size and organisation of the economic agents, existing policies and regulation governing that sector, its economic significance, international dimension etc.

Transport, energy and agriculture are three economic sectors of particular environmental relevance. Therefore, the possible role of economic instruments and the constraints and issues which ought to be taken into consideration for applying economic instruments to these sectors are briefly reviewed in this section.

Sectoral considerations are also crucial for improving the integration between environmental policy and policies applied to specific economic sectors.

Although "industry" is not an economic sector as such, some considerations are also given about the application of economic instruments, as industrial plants and organisations constitute major pollution sources.

4.1   Transport

i)   Background issues

Transport is a sector where, although economic instruments have not in the past played a major role in environmental policy, there is a gradual increase in their use. It is also an important sector in terms of its scale and growth, and environmental intrusion is a continuing problem.

While much of the environmental degradation associated with transport can be traced to inadequacies in transport markets, to fully internalize all costs it is also important to correct for intervention failures. These occur when governments manipulate transport markets to achieve regional, industrial, social and other policy objectives without taking full account of the environmental costs involved. Such intervention failures occur in many sectors but, because of the central role transport plays in economic development, it is particularly prone to them. The diversity of environmental effects associated with transport also means that intervention failures may occur because of conflicts in the application of a variety of environmentally orientated policy instruments which counteract one another.

Traditionally, command and control instruments such as regulations and licences have been the tools most relied upon to contain the adverse environmental effects of transport.

While the range of regulations which have been employed is extensive they have not achieved many of the environmental objectives for which they were initially employed. In a sense, therefore, economic instruments may, in addition to their natural advantages, be seen as necessary to support the command and control regime which exists.

Until recently, the limited use of economic instruments has mainly taken the form of subsidies to less environmentaly damaging modes (especially public transport) although more recently differential tax systems have been initiated in some OECD countries. These relate to such matters as differential tax regimes by vehicle size, sometimes environmental characteristics and to tax differentials on the fuels used in transport. Economic instruments have also been deployed to reinforce regulatory measures (e.g. fiscal incentives to accelerate the legal compliance with standards). In addition to new initiatives, it is necessary that these types of economic instrument are further developed and deployed more widely.

Transport interfaces with many other sectors where environmental policy is important (e.g. energy and industry). It is vital, therefore, that the policies applied in the transport sector are consistent with and, where possible, reinforce the instruments deployed in these other sectors. Economic instruments can play a major role in this respect.

ii)   *The Role of economic instruments*

In a sector embracing a range of alternative technologies, economic instruments are more flexible than regulations. This is particularly true where users, as is frequently the case, have a variety of options open to them, enabling adjustments to be made in an efficient manner. Transport users, for example, when confronted by economic stimuli often have the options of travelling as before but paying for the environmental damage they cause, reducing their travel, retiming their trips, rerouting their trips, changing transport mode, or of technically modifying the existing mode. In the long term there is the further option of relocation. The empirical evidence on elasticities is that users are more likely to modify their behaviour when confronted with fiscal incentives than with regulatory controls.

In the longer term economic instruments also encourage the development of new technologies and modifications to existing technologies which ultimately add to the overall environmental improvement. Fuel surcharges (e.g. a carbon tax) reflecting the global warming effects of CO_2 emissions, for instance, would not just result in economy in the use of fuels by the existing vehicle fleet but also stimulate research into more fuel efficient engines to reduce the need to pay these surcharges.

Regulations have a role to play in transport where the transactions costs (including enforcement) of applying economic instruments is high. This applies in many areas relating to safety (e.g. road engineering standards, airport design, etc), but may also be applicable to problems of community severance (which is complicated with issues involving land use planning). Regulations are also important with regard to the transport of hazardous materials.

iii)   *Type of economic instruments*

Emissions charges

Well established systems of registration make it viable to charge for **noise** created by aircraft, motor vehicles and public transport according to the specific accoustic characteristics of the transport involved. Because of their freedom to use the entire road network, national standards may be necessary for motor vehicles, but with aircraft or rail services the charges should be adjusted to meet local and regional conditions (See Section 3.4).

Given the problems of monitoring **air pollution** from motor vehicles, and enforcement difficulties, atmospheric pollution is often most effectively dealt with through product charges (see below). In some cases where emissions and product charges are not viable, annual vehicle licence fees and taxation on vehicle purchases could be related to the nature of the vehicle concerned (e.g. its size, power unit, age, etc). In practice, noise and air pollution charges on motor-vehicles could be combined, e.g. in the form of an annual vehicle tax related to vehicle characteristics, and/or a special fuel tax, to take into account actual vehicle use.

Product charges

The diffuse nature and mobility of sources of transport pollution means product charges on inputs should play an important practical role in environmental policy. They should be seen to be acting as surrogates for emissions charges and, by influencing the costs of inputs into the transport sector, act upon the final output of emissions.

Fuels used in transport should be subjected to charges reflecting the ultimate environmental damage caused. Tax differentials between leaded and unleaded fuels are increasingly common as are tax differentials between gasoline and diesel. These types of differential should be further developed and modified as knowledge of the respective environmental costs of alternatives expand. Differentials should reflect as near as possible the full environmental costs of the alternatives.

In the case of lead, benzene, etc. the relevant rates, because of the domestic nature of the environmental problems involved in these cases should be set by State or national authorities. Where there are transfrontier spillovers, as with NO_x emissions, national governments should adjust their product charges to fully reflect these.

Carbon taxes could also be introduced to combat problems of global warming. These should extend to all modes for transport to ensure both internal efficiency within the transport sector and to contain the emissions of modes which have static sources of power (e.g. electric locomotion). Carbon taxes applied to transport modes should be part of a carbon tax on all fuel burning. The application should be by international agreement and at a common global rate to reflect the nature of the costs involved, (see Section 5.2).

Product charges may also apply to vehicles, i.e. according to their environmental characteristics in terms of emissions, fuel consumption etc.

Product taxes may gainfully be used in combination with other forms of policy instrument. In particular, they should be considered as a means of accelerating the adoption of legal standards (such as the introduction of catalytic convertors) or of going beyond these standards.

Charges may be developed in such a way that they are revenue-neutral (See Section 1). This is possible by combining surcharges and discounts. For example, differential rates on leaded and unleaded gasoline may be developed in this way.

Deposit-refund systems

Transport vehicles contain substantial amounts of recycleable materials together with quantities of non-biodegradeables (e.g. plastics) and toxic matter (e.g. in batteries). Additionally, inappropriate disposal of transport hardware (both vehicles and infrastructure) is unsightly. Because of the ease of imposition and the benefits of ensuring appropriate disposal, automobiles, trucks, aircraft and other pieces of transport equipment are highly amenable to refundable deposit schemes and these should be more widely used. Further, by allowing liquidisation of an asset through the reclaiming of the refund, such schemes encourage a more rapid removal of older, more environmentally intrusive vehicles from the fleet.

Schemes should be at the national level, or even international level, to discourage excessive movement of scrap within countries and be designed so as to reflect the material composition of different vehicle classes.

Derelict transport infrastructures (e.g. old docks, canals, rail yards, etc) are visually intrusive and can be dangerous. Deposit refund schemes (in the form of bonds) could be used to ensure that those responsible for transport infrastructure (irrespective of whether it is publicly or privately provided) rehabilitate contaminated soil and return sites to their former state at the end of the life of the infrastructure. Such schemes should be local in their orientation.

Marketable permits

The nature of transport means that market solutions involving the allocation of property rights over the environment is seldom a practical policy option. Frequently, and especially with regard to the pollution caused by the automobile, both the number of individuals adversely affected and the number of those responsible for the damage is considerable. Individual trading of environmental rights is difficult in such cases. Even where the perpetrator of the damage is clearly identifiable (e.g. a ship or aircraft), the number of individuals adversely affected again makes trading solutions impractical in most cases. However, such approaches may be envisaged in the case of averaging fuel economy standards and heavy duty truck engine emission standards in the United States.

There are also some limited instances where these issues are less severe. In the case of reducing some toxics (e.g. lead) from fuels, tradeable rights could be used at the refining stage to ensure that reductions are made in the economically most efficient manner. Similarly, they could be used at the vehicle manufacturing stage with regard to assisting in the most cost-effective means of reducing the use of plastics, acids, etc.

Other charges with environmental implications

Many of the adverse effects of transport are highly correlated with congestion. Congestion itself results in a direct deterioration in the environment of those caught in it but it also inevitably generates increased atmosperic pollution and possibly noise.

Congestion is caused by a misperception on the part of transport users of the costs they impose on other transport users. Congestion charges which make transport users aware of these costs will also generally lead to a reduction in other forms of environmental damage. Road pricing is a special case of congestion charging which relates to urban congestion and its implementation would generate both transport and environmental gains. Congestion charges would also prove beneficial at airports. They should be determined at the local level.

Additional to the need for congestion charges is the requirement that the fixed (e.g. annual licence fees, purchases taxes, etc) and variable (e.g. fuel duty, tolls etc) charges imposed on transport users reflect the fixed and variable costs they impose (including all environmental costs). An excessive loading on the fixed element of charging, often done for fiscal convenience, can lead to an excessive use of transport with associated adverse environmental implications. This "variabilisation" of car cost could be usefully developed.

Subsidies

Direct subsidies may serve a limited purpose in the transport sector when used to rehabilitate areas left derelict after transport infrastructure becomes redundant (e.g. dock areas, rail alignments etc). Since these are essentially legacy effects, there is no opportunity for the application of the Polluter-Pays-Principle.

iv)   **Practical and policy implementation issues**

Acceptability

Transport is visible and impinges on many aspects of everyday life and many productive activities. The adoption of economic instruments in the transport field will, therefore, affect a diverse range of transport users and also many who, for reasons of access, rely on transport by others. Acceptability of such measures will critically depend upon those affected being fully informed of the rationale of the measures and the ultimate benefits to be reaped. For distributional reasons it may be important that some groups disadvantaged by the use of economic instruments be adequately compensated and to introduce such economic instruments in the framework of a global tax reform (e.g. revenue neutral).

Suppliers of transport hardware (including both vehicles and infrastructure), together with oil companies and other suppliers of energy, will be affected by the introduction of economic instruments. These bodies need time to adjust their production plans and technologies in order to respond efficiently and with minimum disruption to the new situation. For acceptance, adequate prior warning of the imposition of economic instruments is therefore necessary. Overall, the introduction of economic instruments, because of the stimuli they provide for incorportating cleaner technology on vehicles, greater recycling of materials and, in the short term, an acceleration of fleet replacement, will not have a serious adverse effect on vehicle manufacturers.

Transport is already subjected to a variety of charges and taxes in all OECD countries, as well as receiving substantial amounts of subsidy. For public acceptance it is important that the exact nature of any environmentally based charge is transparent and that those liable to pay are aware of its nature. It should not be seen as a further form of general taxation aimed purely at revenue raising.

Coordination

A specific feature of transport is the diversity of environmental effects it creates. In introducing economic instruments to the transport sector, it is important that measures are coordinated to prevent potential government intervention failures arising. The wide range of environmental matters to be tackled will require the application of a range of instruments and without coordination some may prove counterproductive. Coordination between the various agencies and bodies involved in different aspects of environmental policy is essential.

It is also important that the economic instruments applied to transport interface appropriately with those deployed in related sectors (e.g. land use planning, energy, industry, etc).

Information

The large number of polluters involved in land transport (especially motor vehicle users) means that the impact of economic instruments will be widespead across the population. Their adoption, therefore, should be accompanied by appropriate educational and consultation programmes. These should explain the need for concerted action with regard to transport and especially highlight not simply the local benefits of adopting economic instruments (especially with regard to noise) but also the longer term, global benefits which are often not fully perceived at present. It is also important that information and up-dates are provided on a continuous basis rather than simply when some policy change is being proposed.

In many cases it may be possible to introduce economic instruments, at least initially, in a tax neutral way. For example, greater emphasis on use related charges and lesser reliance on period fees and charges. This should be made clear to those affected and, where necessary, to the fiscal authorities.

Consultation

With regard to some sectors (notably aviation, shipping and rail transport) suppliers are relatively concentrated and consultation should involve them either directly or through their representative bodies in discussion over the nature of the economic policy instruments to be deployed and over detailed questions of implementation.

Consultation with users of transport, including motorists who act as suppliers and consumers, should be as widespread as possible with a very high degree of information dissemination and education embraced within it. In particular, it is important that not only the policy options available at the time of implementation be fully considered but that the possibility of longer term developments be pointed out and reviewed.

Costs

The application of economic instruments to transport is not costless. For instance, it impose short term costs on users of transport, costs on manufacturers of transport hardware who have to re-tool and, by affecting the relative attractiveness of different locations, imposes costs on certain land-owners. Acceptability may require designing instruments in such a way that some of these costs are minimised (e.g. via revenue neutral means) although ultimately it must be recognized that economic instruments are intended to make transport users aware on the environmental costs they impose.

There are also transactions costs involved in introducing, enforcing and administrating systems of economic instruments. When deciding upon, first, the benefits of adopting policies to contain the environmental impacts of transport and, second, the merits of economic instruments as opposed to alternatives these transactions costs should be considered. Because there is an established tradition and administrative framework for imposing taxes on transport users (e.g. fuel taxation) the transaction costs of extending these to embrace environmental costs should be low.

Enforcement

The application of economic instruments in the transport sector should be seen to be fair in the sense that avoidance or evasion is difficult. Because of the large number of users of transport and the mobility of the polluting sources, effective enforcement of environmental policies with regard transport can be difficult and costly (e.g. as is seen with regulations regarding speed limits, urban parking, noise limits, etc).

In considering which economic instruments to deploy it is thus important that full costing be made of the alternatives including the costs of monitoring and enforcement. These costs should be allowed for prior to the initiation of any policy in the transport sector. In some cases it may be necessary to sacrifice a degree of efficiency, in terms of the theoretical outcome of using a particular policy, if the transactions costs of implementation are in practice very high. Because of the smaller number of parties involved product charges may be prefered to emissions charges in the case of motor vehicle traffic for this reason.

Enforcement must involve severe penalties for those who attempt to avoid payment of environmental charges.

Economic and distributive consequences

Both the use of economic instruments and regulations to reduce environmental degradation ultimately affect the costs of using transport. This means that in addition to affecting the wealthy, they affect groups on low incomes (e.g. the elderly, unemployed, etc) although the degree of hardship imposed will be influenced by the travel patterns of these groups. They also affect different individuals in various ways according to where they live and firms according to where they are located (e.g. firms distant from their markets will pay relatively more in transport costs).

Imposing charges on those responsible for environmental damage generates revenue which can be used for compensation purposes, in the case of low income groups, or to ease transition in cases where relocation may be felt important. Policies designed to use the revenues from economic charges to assist disadavantaged groups should be developed prior to introducing economic instruments and these groups should be informed of these.

Earmarking of revenues generated by the application of economic instruments may also be deployed as a means of financing complementary environmental actions in the transport sector (e.g. provision of noise barriers, insulating buildings, by-pass construction, tunnels, etc.). Such complementary actions should be subjected to full cost-benefit appraisal prior to adoption.

Priorities

Given the diversity of transport markets, the number of vested interests who enjoy free ridership under current conditions, and the range of environmental issues involved, it is important that an order of priority is established selecting initially those areas for the introduction of economic instruments where the greatest demonstrable benefits will materialise.

The pronounced impact of differential charges on leaded and unleaded gasoline, for example, illustrates the potential for extending fiscal incentives of this type to embrace other environmentally damaging components of fuels used in transport (e.g. benzene). Refundable deposit schemes related to the materials which are contained in motor vehicles would have an immediate positive effect on the level of visual blight associated with scrapped vehicles and would rapidly encourage greater efforts at recycling.

4.2   Energy

i)   *Background*

The energy sector covers a wide variety of activities in the economy, energy being both an intermediate as well as a final product. Both production and consumption of energy have environmental impacts. The most prominent residuals are air pollutants caused by the burning of fossil fuels. These include carbon dioxide, sulphur oxides, nitrogen oxides, particulate matter and a number of potentially toxic pollutants, including heavy metals. Other residuals include water pollutants - conventional and potential toxins - and solid and hazardous waste material. Further, there is a constant danger of oil spills and blow outs associated with the production or the transport of oil, natural gas and refined products. Strip mining of coal imposes a problem of the rehabilitation of the affected area, in addition to enormous volumes of solid waste from coal production. As forests absorb CO_2 and burned wood emits CO_2, the use of wood fuels contribute to increasing CO_2 levels in the atmosphere if the rate of deforestation exceeds the rate of growth of the world's forests. Nuclear energy is considered to be rather "clean", although there is a potential for huge and long term environmental damage if accidents occur. Also, with increased use of nuclear energy, the question of where to deposit nuclear wastes will need to be resolved. Even alternative fossil sources of energy (hydro-, wind-, solar-power) as well as the transmission of electricity, impose environmental damage, however, mainly by scaring the landscape.

The focus of this section is on economic instruments for the reduction of energy related air pollution, this kind of pollution being the most dominant of energy related environmental damage and having characteristics unique to the energy sector.

Large upward and downward variations in the price of oil have shown that the energy sector is quite adaptable to exogenous changes. Also, a number of economic instruments have been applied in the energy sector, such as various energy taxes, tax breaks and subsidies. This experience has shown that supply and demand for various forms of energy are responsive to price changes and that economic instruments can alter behaviour in the energy sector.

The energy sector is closely linked to other sectors - particularly transport and industry -and thus it is important to integrate environmental policies. For example, transportation policies with respect to intermodal travel clearly should be integrated with pollution standards for vehicles.

Economic instruments can help to integrate environmental policy by avoiding the exclusive use of the sectoral approach. Setting the same set of emission charges or creating a single marketable permit system can avoid inconsistencies among sectors and avoid the difficulties of having to set a myriad of environmental regulations. Moreover, adopting an economic incentive scheme that applies across sectors increases its cost-saving potential because that potential is dependent more on variations in cost-effectiveness among pollution sources than among sectors.

ii)   The Role of economic instruments

The energy sector consists of many different actors including both producers and consumers. Therefore, a regulatory approach requires a large and rather detailed apparatus of regulations, rules and standards in addition to an effective monitoring and control system. Broadly based economic instruments, on the contrary, can be designed to affect the relevant groups in the economy by creating incentives which should result in changing behaviour. As all forms of energy have some kind of impact on the environment, economic instruments leading to less production and consumption of energy should lead to less environmental impact. This, however, has to be evaluated with regard to economic growth objectives in general and other sectoral goals. Even without reducing the total production and use of energy, economic instruments should aim at optimizing the fuel mix with regard to reducing environmental damage.

Economic instruments can have different purposes. Economic instruments can be used for revenue raising; however, in the context of environmental policy this is only relevant if the revenue would be earmarked for environmental purposes. The focus here, therefore, is on economic instruments aimed at providing incentives and changing behaviour. Thus, economic instruments can be used to achieve a proper pricing of energy resources, reflecting the true scarcity cost of different types of energy. Further, they can be used to internalize external effects reflecting the full opportunity costs of relevant activities. Thus, they provide incentives for the reduction of emissions and for more efficient use of energy which also should reduce emissions and other environmental damage.

iii)   Types of economic instruments

Emission charges

Presently, there are very few directly energy-related emission charges among the economic instruments in place in OECD countries. To perform effectively as an emission charge, the charge should be based upon the amount of pollution produced thus reflecting environmental damages. It should be levied on actual emissions, which distinguishes it from a product charge (to be discussed later). Thus, for example, a SO_2 tax would be an emission charge on the amount of SO_2 actually emitted. A sulphur tax, on the other hand, would be a product charge imposed on the sale of products containing sulphur, which turns into SO_2 when the product is burned (A sulphur tax would thus be applied before emissions actually occur.). Consequently, the emission charge to be paid could be reduced if less pollution is generated (due to less use of the polluting material or due to the installation of abatement equipment).

Further, it is important that the emission charge as such used as an incentive charge, and the marginal emission charge especially, are large enough to affect a firm's or other economic agent's decision-making. Imposing an emission charge requires that emissions are measured and/or monitored by regular and/or sample surveys. Thus, emission charges can become quite costly. However, there is a possibility of levying a maximum emission charge for all polluters which can be reduced gradually when firms **prove** that they emit less pollution.

Sulphur and nitrogen charges are examples of emission charges. Both CO_2- and sulphur-emissions depend on the fuel mix as such and the fuels' sulphur and carbon content respectively, both of which are variable. As CO_2 cannot readily be removed, a CO_2-charge should aim at reduced and more efficient use of fossil fuels in general and a shift away from carbon based fuels. A sulphur charge induces the polluter either to change to substitutes with a lower sulphur content or to install cleaning equipment.

It is, however, difficult to know exactly the size of the emission charge which is necessary to achieve the desired reduction in emissions. However, if the initially chosen charge does not seem appropriate, it could be adjusted later. The adaptation process in the energy market would result in the individual actors reducing their emissions as long as their marginal costs of reduction are lower than the charge, halting the reduction when marginal costs are equal to the charge. Thus, the size of the reduction of emissions would differ, but the marginal cost of reduction would be equal for everybody and equal to the charge.

The nitrogen oxides formed during combustion do not emanate solely from the nitrogen content in the fuel, but also result from a reaction between the oxygen and nitrogen present in the atmosphere in conjunction with combustion. Consequently, the nitrogen oxides differ in principle from other pollutants from combustion, which are mostly dependent on the composition of the fuel. Accordingly, a charge on nitrogen oxides could be designed as an emission charge and be based on direct measurements of nitrogen emissions from combustion. However, the cost of measuring such emissions can be relatively substantial and might be a restriction for the charge. If this is the case, it is most suitable to levy a charge on nitrogen oxides only on large utilities, notwithstanding appropriate control measures on smaller utilities.

Product charges

As there is a strong correlation between fuel characteristics and polluting emissions, product charges are a useful proxy for emission charges.

Fuels (oil, coal, peat) can be charged/taxed according to their sulphur content. Reduction in the charge should be granted when sulphur content is reduced by means such as flue gas desulphurisation.

Emissions of carbon dioxide are dependent on the carbon content of fuels. Since there are no technically and economically feasible means for capturing and removing CO_2 from flue gases, emissions can only be reduced by a rational choice of fuel and energy-efficient combustion, or less combustion.

A product charge would be applied on the purchase of a "polluting" product. In the case where a product charge is levied as a proxy for emission charges, however, the product charge, in contrast to the emission charge per se, is imposed before emissions arise. On the other hand, a product charge would exempt emissions arising before the purchase of a product (e.g. the flaring of natural gas on the field increases the level of carbon dioxide in the atmosphere, but would not be covered by a product charge on oil or natural gas).

As they are imposed on products, product charges are suitable to differentiate between substitutable products and so are particularly appropriate for fuels. Charges can be differentiated according to the impact on the environment of the production and/or consumption of products. Consequently, the consumer can be influenced in the choice of products. Thus, a higher charge on leaded fuel than unleaded fuel is an example of a successful product charge which has been introduced in many OECD countries.

However, the effect of a product charge depends crucially on the elasticity of demand and the availability of less polluting products (see Chapter II). A product charge is effective when it increases the relative price of polluting products notably and if the consumer has a choice between more or less producing products.

Marketable permits

Emissions of sulphur, nitrogen oxides and carbon dioxide may be susceptible for trading schemes. The crucial element in a system with marketable permits is the initial allocation of these permits, as well as how the total number of permits is restricted and/or reduced over time. Further, the size of a market for this trade has to be sufficient to allow for competition and "real" trade. As for charges, the costs of monitoring can be substantial and have to be considered in such a concept. If the trade in permits works well, permits will be traded as long as marginal costs of reduction of emissions differ. A system with tradeable emission permits will have the same effect with regard to cost efficiency as a system with emission charges (see Chapter II).

iv)   ***Target groups***

The energy sector consists, as mentioned, of many different actors, including both producers and consumers of intermediate and final energy. Therefore, economic instruments in the energy sector have to be employed and adjusted in order to affect the relevant target group in the most efficient way.

Regarding emissions of carbon dioxide, sulphur and nitrogen oxides certain aspects of the energy sector are characterised by few, large sources of emission (e.g. electricity generating plants and refineries, but disregarding emissions in the transport sector, heating in houses and other discharges, which are small in size but numerous). The relatively small number of polluting sources in certain sectors of stationary sources makes monitoring and other administrative constraints for implementing economic instruments less burdensome in these parts of the energy sector.

The damage done by various energy-related emissions may vary a great deal depending upon where and when the emissions occur. The importance of these factors varies with the particular pollutant. For greenhouse gases, location is irrelevant, as emissions have the same effect regardless of where they occur. Depending on weather conditions acid rain can affect areas far away form its sources. In contrast, concerning photochemical oxidants and smog, ozone precursors (nitrogen oxides and hydrocarbons) have very different effects depending upon the source; sources in highly polluted urban areas lead to high ozone concentrations while those in rural areas have very little effect.

Economic instruments should therefore be targeted for maximum advantage. For global warming, trading systems or taxes should be coordinated on a global basis for maximum costs savings. But for most other environmental problems, utilities and other energy producers can face different incentives depending upon where their emissions occur.

v)   ***Practical and policy implementations issues***

As a general principle one should try to introduce the fewest number of **different** economic instruments in the same sector or for the same target groups as possible in order to avoid overlapping or loop holes and to minimize administrative costs.

Economic instruments must also take into account administrative feasibility and the likely technological options for control. Since energy production facilities - most notable electric power plants - tend to be large sources with well-monitored emissions, that aspect of the energy sector is easier to include in a program based on emission charges. But there are some small sources - such as cogenerators or small utilities - that would be difficult to include in a system. For these sources, a scheme targeted on fuel use rather than emissions may be superior. For example, the government could issue permits - or impose taxes - to fuel distributors based upon expected emissions from each fuel. These small sources could get credits (or rebates) if they showed reduced emissions from installing technology. Particularly if the technological options were relatively unimportant, this targeting of fuel would help reduce emissions by encouraging cost-effective conservation and switching to low-emitting fuels.

Economic instruments such as product charges are more efficient where one has many sources of pollution; for few sources emission charges (or even standards) can be used.

However, the effect of any of the discussed economic instruments will be weakened or even reversed as long as contradicting incentives (namely subsidies) for the same target groups are not removed and work at cross purposes.

Economic and distributive consequences

Emission reductions will impose costs on individual actors and on the economy. Comparing the cost effectiveness of different economic instruments permits governments to choose the most cost efficient ones. However, imposing any economic instrument in environmental policy one has to consider its possible effects on economic growth in general, as well as the expected effects on global climate, people's health, safety, etc.

In theory, both charges and marketable permits will result in the same pattern or allocation of the reduction of emissions. Economic instruments can have different distributional impacts - among firms, consumers, and the government - depending on how they are structured. Electric utilities and other energy producers and their customers could thus be affected differently. Any instrument based on a product's carbon content, for example, all else being equal will tend to reduce coal production, thus "hurting" coal producers, and tend to increase production of fuels with lower carbon content, thus "helping" the producers of natural gas and possibly oil.

Charges and permits sold or auctioned by the government will obviously increase the sector's costs, as the charges have to be paid or permits to be bought for the volume of emissions. However, firms whose marginal costs of abatement are lower than the charge or the price of a permit will be affected less than those with higher marginal costs.

If permits are tradeable all firms can gain (compared to a "no-trade-situation") as long as marginal costs of reductions of emissions differ, and markets function properly.

Finally, one should not forget that incentives for the use of non-fossil energy and the installation of cleaning equipment gives growth impulses to those sectors of the economy.

4.3   Agriculture

i)   *Background issues*

Agriculture has a strong impact on environmental quality. This is due to the fact that agricultural production is the most important land use in terms of land area and is altering ecological interrelationships within nature itself.

The environmental impact of agriculture can be positive as well as negative. Farming may for example improve as well as destroy the fertility of soils or the diversity of biotopes and species. Agriculture, thereby, determines not only the ecological quality but also the aesthetic appeal of the rural countryside.

Any assessment of the environmental impact of agriculture therefore involves more than the mere measurement of ecological parameters. It also reflects social value judgements.   The manner in which certain environmental effects are interpreted is influenced by individual cultural traditions. They differ from region to region and may change with time, depending on such factors as population density, the state of economic development or the degree of self-suffciency in food. The relative importance of different environmental issues - such as soil erosion, water pollution, habitat loss or rural amenity - will vary too.

Whatever the conclusion might be - if the relationship between agriculture and the environment is seen more as one of harmony or one of conflict - there can be no doubt about the need to internalize positive as well as negative externalities. This is even more urgent, since the dramatic structural transformation of agriculture during the last few decades has, on balance, undermined many favourable farming practices, aggravated long existing environmental threats and created many new problems.

Some of the major concerns of environmental policy in agriculture are related to the conservation and protection of:

-- soils against erosion, compaction, salinization and pollution caused by nutrients and pesticides etc.;

-- water - groundwater, surface water, drinking water etc. - against eutrophication and other kinds of pollution (e.g. pesticide residues);

-- air against emissions like ammonia from livestock waste or straw burning;

-- biotopes and wildlife habitats against reductions in size and disturbance of their ecological balance (e.g. eutrophication);

-- countryside (rural landscapes) against changes endangering their recreational value and cultural heritage.

The complexity of environmental problems caused by modern agriculture can be considered from two perspectives:

-- One aspect is the expansion or reduction in the area of land used for agricultural production (e.g.: conversion of grass-land, drainage of wetland, fallow, set-aside, abandonment).

-- The other aspect is the intensification and specialisation of agricultural production (e.g.: increase in stocking densities, fertilizer and pesticide use, reduced diversity of rotations and crop varieties).

Both these tendencies are strongly interrelated. Politically they cannot be tackled separately. What makes it even more difficult is that all these structural changes do not happen in the same way at all locations. The process of structural transformation and environmental degradation is characterized rather by regional polarization leading to inter-regional differentiation - between favourable and less-favoured areas - and to intra-regional uniformation - monoculture and monotony - at the same time. Therefore, any assessment and policy in the field of agriculture and the environment has to take due account of the great regional differences and the diverging trends in the various rural areas.

Environmental problems related to agriculture are typically of a 'non-point'-nature (erosion, pollution from fertilizers and pesticides). Agriculture is characterized by a large number of relatively small production units, and due to the specific technological characteristics of farming there are many interfaces between the ecological, technological and socio-economic spheres. This is, why agriculture cannot easily be controlled directly, if ever.

With the exception of complete bans - e.g. on pesticides causing health hazards - direct environmental regulation is in most cases almost impossible to implement. The use of economic instruments, on the other hand, seems to be particularly appropriate. Nevertheless, up to now there have only been a few instances where economic incentives have been used explicitly for environmental purposes in agriculture.

Even worse, traditional measures of agricultural support policy have for a long time distorted relative prices and thereby given economic incentives not only to over-production, but also to an environmentally damaging over-use of land, an over-intensification in the use of polluting chemicals and an over-specialisation in certain products not only on the farm level, but also for whole regions.

Today, most OECD countries are confronted with problems of a highly subsidised surplus-production causing budgetary tensions and international trade conflicts (GATT). These problems urgently demand a new orientation of agricultural policy anyhow. This provides a good opportunity for a better integration of environmental considerations into the design of new agricultural policy measures.

ii)   *The Role of economic instruments*

Economic instruments and direct regulation

Agriculture is subject to different kinds of direct environmental and health regulations. Agro-chemicals, feed-additives, growth hormones etc., are subject to various kinds of standards. They have to be licensed and are sometimes banned completely. Planning laws and zoning regulations are other important tools of environmental regulation. In some cases drainage, conversion from grass to arable land, manure application or mowing of grass in certain periods, straw burning etc. is either forbidden or requires special permits.

Quite often, however, the regulatory approach is difficult to adopt or to enforce. Here, economic incentives can plan an important role in speeding up compliance, as a complement to or even as a substitute for standards.

Integration of agricultural and environmental policy

The key problem with agricultural markets is, however, that these are not at all "free" markets, but often strongly protected. In most countries, economic instruments are used as means of a sectoral food and farm policy, in order to secure self-sufficiency, to promote food-exports and to increase farm incomes.

As a result, agricultural policy has quite often created major distortions in agricultural price relations, thereby placing severe strains not only on markets and budgets, but also on the environment. It is therefore an important task to achieve a better integration of environmental and agricultural policy.

The present debate on a reorientation of agricultural policy in many OECD countries provides a good opportunity to review the existing support schemes in the light also of their environmental impact. This may then result in proposals

-- to correct certain price support mechanisms that favour environmentally harmful practices;

-- to improve targeting of supply management schemes, like set-aside or extensification programmes, in order to make them environmentally more effective;

-- to make certain income aids and other payments dependent on compliance with conservation and protection demands ("Cross-compliance").

Unless distortions created by agricultural policy measures are reduced, economic instruments to achieve environmental goals will be more expensive, because they will have to offset the negative allocational effects of sectoral support. Charges, subsidies or compensation payments will have to be higher than they would otherwise be.

A transformation of price and trade distorting sectoral support measures into types of environmental incentives consistent with the Polluter-Pays Principle might also help to open up scope for political compromises in international trade negotiations.

iii)   *Types of economic instruments and selection criteria*

There is a long list of possible economic instruments applicable to agricultural production in order to reduce pollution, to avoid other damage or to promote practices friendly to the environment.

As agriculture causes positive as well as negative externalities, the search for economic instruments cannot focus only on pollution control measures like charges, but must at the same time look for positive incentives like subsidies etc.

However, it is often a difficult task to make a clear distinction between

--   refraining from environmental degradation which, for example, should be brought about by charges, and

--   providing positive environmental services that might merit subsidisation.

"Codes of Good Farming Practice" could be helpful in defining such a borderline. Due to the great variety in natural and structural conditions, such general guidelines will, however, always have to be interpreted and adopted according to regional or even local conditions.

Charges/taxes

Charges always have a double effect. They act as an incentive to change behaviour and they raise funds. In agriculture, incentive charges could mainly be used either to reduce pollution damage or to prevent the conversion of land to other - more intensive - uses.

Due to the specific characteristics of agricultural of production (small size, non-point-sources), emissions - such as run-off or leaching of nutrients or other active ingredients - as well as immissions of pollutants into soils, water, air or habitats are almost impossible to control. However, as pollution damage - on-site as well as off-site - is mostly caused by the use of certain inputs (like fertilizers, feedstuffs, pesticides, growth regulators etc.), the easiest way to implement pollution charges seems to be the application of a **product charge** on those inputs.

In addition, one could think about charges levied on those hectares of arable land which are not under a "green cover" in autumn. Such crop covers can help to reduce the risk of erosion as well as of nitrogen-leaching from bear soils during the winter.

Conversion charges could be considered for activities like drainage, ploughing-up of grass-land, removal of landscape features such as hedges etc. Up to now, however, traditional agricultural policy supports rather the opposite (e.g. drainage, land consolidation).

In several West-European countries, **fertilizer-charges** are a key issue in the present debate on agriculture and the environment. Studies suggest, however, that price elasticities are rather low, so that charge-rates would have to be very high in order to induce major reduction in the intensity of fertilizer use. On the other hand, high charge-rates would cause drastic income losses to farmers. Therefore, fertilizer-charges are in fact only discussed under the assumption that at least part of the revenue is paid back to farmers.

If, for example, the receipts of the charge were paid back at a flat rate per hectare, then in fact only the environmentally damaging **over**-use of fertilizers would be charged and income problems would be a less troublesome factor. However, receipts could also be used to finance subsidies for specific environmental purposes. This could increase the environmental effectiveness of the measure.

Charges on mineral fertilizer seem to be quite easy to administer. It would be more difficult to charge organic fertilizer from animal manure. In this case, stocking densities or feedstuffs could be the right charge base.

Pesticide charges, either on the amount of active ingredients or on the number of treatments, could also help to reduce pollution problems (8).

Subsidies/premia

As a general rule, subsidies are incompatible with the Polluter-Pays Principle except in a few specific cases. However, up to now, subsidies and premia are in the forefront of economic instruments in agriculture. Subsidies are used *inter alia* as:

-- Remuneration for special environmentally beneficial services that go beyond "Good Agricultural Practice" and which would otherwise not be profitable. Such payments aim, for example, at the preservation of traditional production systems or at the maintenance of or change to specific modes of environmentally sound production.

-- Incentives to speed up technological changes towards environmentally sound production methods.

-- Compensation payments for unacceptable costs of adjustment, e.g. to reduce drastic income losses caused by the introduction of pollution charges.

Compensation type subsidies should, however, only be allowed for a limited period of time, in cases where severe difficulties occur. Major distortions in competition should be avoided.

One advantage of subsidies compared to charges is that in many cases they are easier to target according to specific regional or sectoral conditions. On the other hand, subsidies often relate only to existing management techniques. Thus, subsidies may reward those who have been poor performers prior to their introduction and their role as incentives to search for new technologies that could be more effective is less strong.

Charge cum subsidy schemes

Charges cum subsidy schemes provide a good means to combine the advantages of charges and subsidies and, at the same time, to avoid their shortcomings. Such integrated sets of economic instruments could, for example, make use of the strong incentives for induced technological change as well as of the revenue-raising function of charges, but could alleviate their distributional problems. At the same time, they could take advantage of the possibilities of a better targeting of subsidies.

Such schemes could provide a double incentive to reduce environmentally damaging activities: on the one hand, by charges on fertilizers and/or pesticides, on the other hand, by subsidies for extensification measures such as completely abandoning the use of mineral fertilizers, pesticides or growth regulators.

Marketable permits

The distribution of marketable permits one possibility to control pollution in an efficient and effective manner. Again, as pollutants from non-point sources cannot easily be monitored, the economic instruments will have to be oriented towards inputs such as fertilizers and pesticides.

Compared to fertilizer charges, a quota on nitrogen in purchased fertilizers seems to have certain advantages insofar as the desired reduction in the overall intensity could be reached immediately and regardless of fluctuations in price. The total amount of inorganic nitrogen would be assigned to farmers on a hectare base. Its distribution between different locations and crops, as well as the price for quotas, would be determined by the market. Income effects would be similar to those of a nitrogen-charge with reimbursement. Administration should not be too difficult in a sector where many products like milk, sugar, wine etc. are already subject to quota-regimes.

Quota regulations have also been discussed for pesticides. Due to the great variety of different types and application modes, administration and other transaction costs of a quota system seem to be much higher than in the case of fertilizers. Also, the need for pest-control is subject to major annual fluctuations.

Deposit-refund systems

Deposit-refund systems are yet not very important in agriculture. Containers and bottles for agricultural products like milk, wine, juices, eggs etc. can however be subject to such systems. The obligation to collect and clean bottles may be quite burdensome, especially for small farmers, so that one has to think about appropriate institutional arrangements (e.g. cooperatives).

Another field for application of deposit-refund systems would be for pesticide containers. There should also be an obligation or incentive - e.g. refund of pesticide charges - to return remaining residuals that have not been used.

iv)   *Field of operation*

Using economic instruments, one can distinguish at least three different approaches.   Output- or impact-related approaches, input- or source related approaches and finally process-or technology-related technologies.

Output-/impact-related

In the case of pollution control, output-related charges or quota are difficult to apply.   Pollutants from non-point sources are difficult to monitor.   In certain limited areas, however, such as water protection zones etc. or for single farms that have signed special management agreements, one could at least try to measure the nutrient content of the soils.   Charges or subsidies could, for example, be differentiated according to the Nmin content at the end of the vegetation periode because the risk of nitrate-leaching is much higher during winter time.

In the case of subsidies, too, output-, or impact-related, payments may have certain advantages.   If, for example, in management agreements farmers received a subsidy per number of endangered species of fauna and flora found on their fields, then farmers would have a much greater incentive to study the ecological interrelationships and to further improve their management than if they only get compensation payments for the maintenance of certain traditional practices.

Input-/source-related

Instead of charging the leaching or run-off of pollutants directly, it seems to be appropriate to put a charge on those inputs that are most likely to cause pollution risks: fertilizers, pesticides, nutrients in feedstuffs etc.

Process-/technology-related

As it is sometimes difficult in agriculture to identify a well-defined hierarchy of environmental objectives, it might be better not to concentrate too much on a single goal -output or impact.   There are in fact many trade-offs between different environmental demands, so that charges or subsidies that are only concentrated on specific issues can easily create new problems in other spheres.   To avoid this and to leave open various options for future development, it may be better to charge or subsidise production systems or modes of production as a whole.   This also means keeping environmental protection integrated into agriculture as a multi-purpose exercise, instead of promoting "landscape gardening" as a separate business which would result in the creation of "artificial" landscapes.

71

v)   ***Targeting***

Proper targeting of economic instruments for environmental protection is of special importance in agriculture because of the great diversity in structural and regional conditions. It is, however, not the implementation of the instrument, but its impact on the target groups or regions that has to be differentiated.

A uniform charge -e.g. per kg of fertilizer- and a uniform flat-rate reimbursement -e.g. per hectare- would have completely different consequences in intensive areas as compared to marginal areas. Highly intensive farms would be faced with a negative balance between (charge) payments and (refund) receipts whereas extensive farms could even expect a positive revenue. Thus an undifferentiated use of economic instruments, which is easy to handle on the administrative level, can nevertheless result in regionally differenciated incentives at farm level, as it is desired.

Criteria for targeting economic incentives could be **farming characterics** such as farm size, defined either in hectares, in number of stock or in income capacity. For administrative reasons small farms - with less than two or three hectares - are often excluded from policy measures. From an environmental point of view, intensity and type of farming seem to be even more important than farm-size. Charges could, for example, be directed especially towards intensive livestock farms (pig and poultry) with stocking densities far beyond average.

Certain subsidies may only be paid for farms producing according to specific guidelines (e.g. "organic" farming). In those cases, it may often be better to target measures not only to individual farms but also to groups of farms, such as cooperatives or other kind of organisations.

Economic incentives aiming at changes in agricultural production could also focus, however, on **industries and services** outside the agricultural sector. As agriculture today is strongly linked with other related sectors, such as the chemical industry or the food processing industries, it may in some cases be even better to implement measures at their level. For example, the best place to collect fertilizer charges would be fertilizer factories and importers. Users should be explicitly informed of the existence of such environmental charge, for transparency of the system.

As the spatial dimension of environmental problems is particularly important in agriculture, there is often a need for regional and local differentiation. Also in traditional agricultural policies, many instruments apply only in certain areas, such as hill or mountain areas. For environmental purposes, various environmentally

sensitive areas could be designated: e.g. soil-conservation or water-protection zones, nature-conservation sites. The main problem, however, caused by such differentiations is that this leads to different standards in "production"-and "protection"-zones.

vi)   ***Modes of operation***

Charge/subsidy base

There are various options to reduce mineral losses by the use of charges. However, their ecological, economic, social and regional implications are often quite different. Nitrate and phosphate pollution charges can be levied on:

--   **Nitrogen content** (N_{min}) in soils at the end of the vegetation period. Administrative costs of this type of charge are very high. They will therefore only be used in certain protection zones.

--   **Nitrogen and phosphates in commercial fertilizers.** This will induce not only a reduction in the intensity of mineral-fertilizer use, but will also lead to substitution effects, such as reducing the share of nitrogen demanding crops and/or increasing the share of nitrogen fixing plants in rotations. The economic value of animal manure will increase, which may lead to a better distribution.

--   **Animal manure** - perhaps even differentiated according to different types (e.g. solid or liquid). This can mean putting a charge on livestock density per hectare or on stocking rates which exceed a certain limit (e.g. 1.5 or 2 lifestock units per hectare).

--   **Purchased feedstuffs** used in intensive livestock production. This can at the margin effect some shifts towards other stock-keeping technologies, changes in the regional distribution of animal production, and substitution towards mineral-poor feedstuffs.

In the case of **pesticide charges**, the charge base could either be the amount of active ingredients or alternatively the number of treatments recommended under standard application conditions.

In the case of **subsidies**, it is also not easy to choose the right subsidy base. In many countries, for example, subsidies are used to promote investment in manure tanks. Bigger storage capacities should help to avoid spreading of manure during

73

the winter, when leaching is highly probable. There are, however, indications that these investment subsidies have, in some cases at least, been counter-productive, as they provided incentives to change from the traditional - less problematic - techniques of solid-manure to liquid-manure management.

Instead of subsidising "end-of-pipe" technologies (storage capacities), it would often be better to provide incentives to either continue with or change to less harmful production systems. In this case, the definition of the subsidy base becomes more difficult. Often, the conditions to be fulfilled have to be described in a detailed contract ("management agreement").

Another important question is whether subsidies should only be paid to farmers who **change** to environmentally beneficial practices, or whether those farmers who have already applied sound techniques over a long period should have the same right to support. This is of importance, for example, in the case of support schemes for "organic" farming.

The wide range of possible options clearly shows that any choice has to be based on careful analysis of the likely impact. Due to the complex interrelationships in agricultural ecosystems, this is in no sense an easy task.

Charge/subsidy rate

The choice of the "right" charge or subsidy rate is another crucial point in the use of economic instruments. Ideally, the rate should reflect the marginal social costs or benefits caused by the external effect. In practice, this will be difficult to achieve.

Charge and subsidy rates will depend on the desired degree of changes in agricultural production, on substitution and price elasticities. Due to massive price distortions caused by agricultural support measures, rates will often have to be much higher than in an undistorted "free" market situation (9).

To set appropriate subsidy rates is equally difficult. In most management agreements, for example, the rate is calculated on the basis of previous income. Payments are therefore no more than just a compensation for losses caused by certain restrictions. This, however, does not really create an incentive to change production in the desired direction. It would therefore be better to devise a method of remuneration taking account not only of the costs, but also of the demand for environmental services.

Assignment of emission rights

The clear definition, assignment and enforcement of rights and duties is a prequisite for any market to behave effectively. This particularly true of new markets created for pollution permits or environmental services with a "public good" character.

For the same reasons that apply to the use of pollution charges, emission rights cannot directly be attached to pollutants either. Input quota could, however, be an effective substitute. As in the case of charges, there are also different ways in which nitrogen quota, for example, could be distributed. Again, it has to be decided whether total nitrogen or only the share of commercial fertilizer should be subject to the quota. Quota could either be distributed as a uniform amount per hectare, or differentiated according to regional conditions. Tradeability of quota would then have to be restricted to certain regions.

vii)   *Implementation and enforcement*

Competence

Competence for agricultural and environmental policies will, in most countries, be with different ministries or departments. There is, however, an urgent need for better integration of both policies. Appropriate institutional structures and procedures should be created for consultation, co-operation and coordination.

Even more difficult than this horizontal integration, is the task of vertical integration of different administrative levels, e.g. international, supra-national, national, regional and local.

Many environmental problems at regional level are caused internationally. Distortions in international markets create problems for certain subnational regions. On the other hand, such regional pollution problems as run-off and leaching of nutrients in intensive livestock areas can have international repercussions, as in the case of North-Sea eutrophication.

In this context, international agreements on general guidelines and rules can play an important role. Drawing up common principles - like the Polluter-Pays Principle - can help to find solutions to a "prisoner's dilemma" where environmental policy measures are not taken because every country would otherwise fear the loss of international competitivity. Such international frameworks should, however, leave sufficient scope for national and regional adaptation. This is particularly true of agriculture, with its great variety according to regional conditions, problems and perspectives.

Regional administrations will have to play a key role in developing concrete answers to the major challenge of agriculture and the environment. Charges, however, are quite difficult to implement at a regional level alone. In the case of subsidies, regional targeting seems to more practical.

Timing

The introduction of economic instruments - especially in the case of charges - should be announced well in advance in order to allow farmers to adjust to the new situation. It will also be necessary to recalculate charge or subsidy rates in the course of time. Charges could, for example, have an initial revenue raising priority. Successively increasing the rate up to the optimum level would then strenghten their incentive function.

Ecological systems demand long periods of adjustment. Thus, environmental policy measures should be implemented in a longer-term perspective. Programmes that support the "set-aside" of land for only one year or the "extensification" of land use for only five years may be effective to reduce surplus problems. For the protection of endangered animal and plant species, such short-term measures are not very effective.

Calculation, invoice, monitoring

The easiest way to apply charges or subsidies is to use a flat rate. If adequate monitoring could be established, other types of calculation (e.g. table-based) would in most cases be better.

Due to the large number of production units, monitoring seems to be almost impossible for public administrations. It seems to be possible only in specific sensitive areas. An alternative way to control compliance would be to keep farmer organisations and/or nature conservation bodies involved. A joint responsibility could also help to overcome traditional sources of conflict and to open a serious dialogue between farmers and nature conservationists.

The management of invoices for environmental charges and subsidies in agriculture will not always require the creation of new administrations. In most countries, there are strong agricultural administrations that have a long tradition in handling economic instruments. It may, however, be necessary to give them new orientations.

Information

Farmers will have to be adequately informed about the seriousness of the environmental problems and their urgent need of solution. They should be aware of the interrelationships between agricultural and environmental policy concerns. They should be informed well in advance about the purpose and the technicalities of the instruments, their timing and financial consequences. Generally speaking, community education has a role to play in order to influence demand and market prices.

Consultation

Farmers and their organisations as well as other competent non-governmental organisations (NGO's), should be able to contribute their competence to the design of the measures. Sometimes, it will even be appropriate to keep them involved in their implementation and administration or to make them responsible for the supervision of the instruments.

Advice

On the other hand, farmers should be provided with sufficient advice about the possibilities for adjustment. This may be either through public teaching and advisory services or through private consultants.

Sector goals

Traditional goals of agricultural policy do not take much account of environmental concerns. In most countries, however, the emphasis has already been shifted towards more environment-oriented goals. The present debate about a reorientation of agricultural policies at international, supranational and national level provides a good opportunity to show that in many cases there is not really a trade-off between "production" and "protection", "development" and "environment".

Distributional goals, such as helping farmers to earn a reasonable income, have always ranked high in agricultural policies. Any economic instrument for environmental protection in agriculture must therefore be assessed not only in the light of efficiency and effectiveness, but should also to be studied with regard to its distributional implications.

Economic instruments should be used in concordance with the general administrative, juridical and fiscal structures and rules. Political and administrative traditions have to be respected. If existing frameworks have to be changed, the introduction of new economic incentives will become much more difficult. The use of economic instruments can in some cases, however, also require institutional innovations.

4.4   Industry

i)   *Background*

Industry is defined as a residual category - as all non-domestic activities which cannot be defined as agriculture, energy and transport. It includes manufacturing and services, and includes non-fuel mineral extraction and power generation for industrial use, but excludes extraction of energy products and utility power generation.

Almost all policy instruments touch the industrial sector directly or indirectly and consequently there is a considerable body of experience in the application of economic instruments to industry throughout the OECD countries. In practice, economic instruments have been applied to the environmental media (discharges to water or air, for example) rather than to the industrial sector as a whole or individual industry sectors. There are a number of reasons mostly linked to the inherent diversity of the industrial sector; it is heterogeneous in terms of size of plant and type of industry, whereas there is greater homogeneity between patterns of discharge from industry (and other dischargers such as municipal treatment plant). These factors affect the use of economic instruments in a number of ways:

--   **Equity.** Many industries discharge similar pollutants (e.g. BOD to water, SO_2 to air); it may be fairer to introduce an economic instruments relative to the discharge rather than individual industry.

--   **Institutional factors.** In the majority of cases, regulatory agencies are established to control pollution on the basis of environmental media. Regulations are designed to control specific waste streams of type of discharge.

-- **Issues of definition**. It may be difficult to identify precisely an individual industrial sector from standard classifications, because of multi-activity plants etc.

Thus, a single economic instrument can be applied to both industry and, say, municipal sewage treatment plants, as in waste water emissions charges; or to both industry and power stations as in the case of SO_2 emissions for large combustion plants.

A second distinguishing feature of the experience of the industrial sector with economic instruments is that instruments applied directly to industry have more frequently taken the form of compensation where requirements for pollution control incurs costs which have been considered unfair or uncompetitively, i.e., subsidies rather than charges.

Where charges are used they have often been offset by a subsidy programme (earmarking of charges and subsidy programmes). This may imply that industry has been successful in modifying pure charging schemes.

A third feature of the industrial sector which distinguishes it from others is its diversity in activity and scale. This means that while economic instruments may impose a financial burden on some industries, the policies behind the instrument may offer new investment and business opportunities for other sectors. Industry has a unique position too in that it pollutes in the production process; the final goods produced by industry may also pollute (e.g. motor-vehicles).

Thus, while the nature of guidelines is to offer general advice, it must be emphasised that the heterogeneity of the sector and the variety of ways in which it pollutes (or contribute to pollution abatement) means that individual subsector responses may vary widely.

Industry may also be particularly responsive to other policy instruments; not only regulation but information, liability and education which impact directly on firms' own responses but also affect directly consumer behaviour and the market. A clear case in point is labelling of environmentally "friendly" products.

ii) *Types of economic instruments criteria for use*

All the main economic instruments can be applied to the industry sector and the general guidelines outlined in Chapter 2 apply. Some particular issues may be noted.

-- Industry may be particularly responsive to requirements to pay the full cost of pollution both through full cost recovery charges for, for example, waste treatment (applicable in cases where full costs have not been effectively passed on to industry); and through strict liability whereby polluters are responsible for damage caused now and in the future. Experience in the United States suggests that this is a particularly powerful tool.

-- **Emission charges** can be applied effectively to industry for water, air pollution and noise. Emission charges can be used where it is technically feasible for industry to reduce its emissions in response to an incentive charge. Incentive charges are an important instrument in encouraging industry to "go beyond" required standards and to develop technologies which move beyond BAT standards.

-- There is considerable scope for **marketable permits**. As well as the more general advantages in overall cost savings attributable to trading, "bubbles" are particularly suited to the concept of Integrated Pollution Control where emissions from a plant are balanced between media as well as by emission. The general conditions and reservations outlined in Chapter 2 also apply.

-- **Deposit-refund systems** have little direct effect on industry but may have a significant indirect impact through influencing consumer behaviour. Industry can be encouraged to set up recycling schemes (e.g. aluminium cans, bottles) by regulatory requirement and deposit-refund schemes can support such initiatives. There is an overlap between deposit-refund schemes and product charges (e.g. if a charge is levied on lubricating oil, it could be refunded if used oil is returned to a reprocessing plant for recycling).

iii)   *Competence and management*

Economic efficiency objectives mean that is important to avoid unnecessary administration and collection costs. There are a number of approaches which can be used to reduce operational costs:

-- **Self-monitoring** by industry. Industry can be required to make regular returns to the administering authority declaring the levels of discharge, with periodical check ups from the regulator. This approach can be linked with other complementary instruments such as **liability** or the

80

requirement to make **information** publicly available about discharges or violation of standards (10).

-- Because of the hetegeroneity of the industrial sector, particularly in terms of size of establishment, smaller dischargers can be charged on the basis of industry coefficients or some other flat rate charge, while larger dischargers can be charged on the basis of actual levels of discharge. This has implications for monitoring requirements.

-- **Use of an existing charging and collection mechanism.** In the case of emission charges, this could mean integrating the collection of the charge with waste water disposal charges. In the case of product or input charges, there are advantages in using an existing tax structure (e.g. value added tax or excise duty).

-- **Linking the charge base with existing standards.** This may allow savings on monitoring which will be required for charges and for regulations. Where the two instruments are used as complements to each other, there is the possibility of shared monitoring costs.

Guidelines appropriate to environmental media are applicable here (see Chapter 3). A properly designed economic instrument should have clear objectives and criteria for evaluation. **Post evaluation** to refine and develop more effective instruments is also essential (but insufficiently done to date) and rests on clear objectives for its validity.

iv)   *Enforcement: acceptability and economic consequences*

Enforcement is concerned with the acceptability of the proposed economic instrument which is regarded as a necessary but not sufficient condition; and the ability to overcome other barriers.

Barriers to acceptability

Acceptance by target groups is a necessary condition if economic instruments are to be effective in economic or environmental terms. However, industry has shown a considerable reluctance to embrace economic instruments, and their case rests on four main issues:

-- Concern that charges impose on additional financial burden;

-- Concern about the use of revenue raised from charges;

-- Belief that economic instruments have no advantage over regulation;

-- Concern about the economic efficiency of charging schemes.

These are, in the main, objections which these guidelines should help to dispel.

Charges as a financial burden

Charges are perceived as a financial burden or penalty in addition to that involved in carrying out pollution abatement to meet regulatory standards. This can result in loss of competitiveness since additional charges are borne ultimately by the consumer, not the industry. This concern is heightened if industry in competitor countries is not subject to the same charges. However, many schemes involve subsidy or a draw back of the charge to support investment in the short term; and as pollution control is introduced, then the level of charge falls. Charges induce in the longer term the implementation of more efficient, less costly, pollution control equipment. This argument is further diluted if revenues raised by charges are redistributed to the sector to support other activities or in reduced charges elsewhere.

Uses of the revenue raised

There is concern about the use of the revenue from charges: either that the revenue might come to be regarded as another source of general taxation revenue and the original objective, which is to control pollution, be forgotten about, or that in the case of redistributive schemes the funds might not be used efficiently or fairly.

Industry generally shows a preference for charge revenues to be channelled back into environmental protection in some way and particularly into measures closely linked with the abatement of the type of pollution being charged for. This is closely tied to the transparency argument, and reflects a fear that the charge will become just another source of general tax revenue, driven by government funding needs rather than environmental objectives. Industry is likely to resist any attempt to introduce a charge that is intended to be solely behaviour-inducing and not redistributive unless this is compensated by an equivalent reduction in other taxation. However, additional worries are that industries not subject to the charge in question might also benefit from such a reduction in taxation and that other sectors e.g. agriculture may benefit.

Many of the "open" redistributive charging schemes have faced the criticism that the link between the charge base and the expenditure is too tenuous. This presents an a priori argument in favour of "closed" charge subsidy schemes which should be tightly focused. This use of subsidies may be acceptable within the framework of the Polluter-Pays-Principle.

Relation with other policy instruments

Industry often claims to prefer regulation to economic instruments. Industry representatives may challenge the efficiency case for economic instruments by arguing that, where regulatory change is foreseen with a time specific objective, say a number of years, industry can optimise its investment planning over time to meet the required standards. Furthermore, a regulatory frameworks allow standards to be raised continuously.

But industry can only optimise on a plant-by-plant basis in respect to regulatory change, whereas economic instruments allow optimisation across the sector. The general case for economic instruments is strong; at a minimum, they reinforce the process already under way through regulatory requirements.

Secondly, in certain specific cases it is believed that economic instruments have no advantages over direct controls. Where there are only a small number of firms discharging a pollutant, industry argues that it is feasible for the regulatory authority to negotiate with all of them on the standards they should reach and measures they should take.

Thirdly, regulations are also preferred in some cases because they offer a level of certainty as to what is required in a way that economic instruments may not. Most charging schemes are directly linked to permits or target standards but their effectiveness also depends on industry's ability to make rational economic responses to the signals offered by the charge. There are some grounds for believing that industry has difficulty in responding except in a rather broad way. There is little evidence that industry knows in any level of detail the costs of pollution abatement it bears, and it appears that few companies have financial appraisal structures which permit a detailed evaluation of the implication of investment and charge level.

Institutional issues

The response to economic instruments will be determined by the institutional context. At a firm level, managers will have a range of objectives for their industry: environment may not be seen as the most important. Economic instruments provide a signal which can help to overcome conservatism and bring environmental investments into the mainstream of corporate planning.

Cultural differences affect responses to the type of economic instruments. In the United States, industry has responded positively to trading but not to charging schemes. In Europe the converse is the case. This reflects the tighter regulatory framework found in the United States, whereby trading has been introduced to add flexibility (and hence reduce costs) in environmental investment. There is generally greater flexibility in regulations and permitting in Europe such that some of the cost savings inherent in trading are already found within the regulatory structure. This is the case in both Germany and the United Kingdom.

Industry responses to economic instruments

When industry groups are opposed to the introduction of economic instruments, their representative groups have taken a number of actions which have included the following both legitimate and illegitimate actions. Legitimately, industry may attempt to stop the instrument from being introduced, or so alter the scheme so that the original objectives are lost sight of and the impact on industry reduced. Industry may challenge schemes on legal grounds, or argue for "special cases", i.e., that every problem is different and needs separate assessment. While theoretically sound, this argument can be a recipe for doing nothing.

Illegitimately, industry may refuse to co-operate, by, e.g. not paying the charges.

Means of overcoming barriers

There are a number of approaches and actions which can either remove the objection or at least facilitate introduction of economic instruments. The emphasis should be on identifying the benefits to industry (e.g. cost savings from trading, new technology, subsidies to help reduce emissions). It will be important to identify clearly the groups which will be beneficiaries as well as those which will lose and focus incentive schemes accordingly, thus taking advantage of the diversity of the industrial sector.

These guidelines have already identified the key factors which are essential in establishing a charging scheme in any sector; equity, simplicity (in order to avoid excessive cost) and transparency. The acceptance of charges will be encouraged if regulatory alternative is more onerous (e.g. a ban on pesticides) and if they have a minimal effect on international competitiveness, and avoid imposing an additional financial burden. Other ways of increasing acceptability are:

-- Use of **carrot and stick**. The availability of subsidies for investment can be used to reinforce the incentive charge. This can also minimise the impact of a charge on an industry sector competitiveness. However, compliance with the Polluer-Pays Principle should be maintained.

-- **Consultation**. This is essential at all stages from the conception of the scheme through to its implementation and evaluation (see also Chapter 2). If industry is consulted first, it can be given the opportunity of suggesting amendments to a proposed scheme. It can be represented on the management board for a scheme; it can be involved in determining appropriate levels of compensation or criteria for charging.

-- **Timing and expectations**. Industry will more readily accept a charging scheme if the physical objectives are clear and the timing of the introduction of the instrument is clear.

-- **Education**. The widespread availability of information about the objectives and need for the use of economic instruments can greatly increase acceptability. This can include advice on how to evaluate the financial and operating implications of economic instruments, particularly for small businesses. Trade associations and Chambers of Commerce have a particularly strong role to play.

Economic consequences

Industry is widely concerned that economic instruments would adversely affect competitiveness and distort prices. A properly designed incentive charge in fact reduces distortions in prices which result from industry's failure to pay its full pollution costs. In international terms, a move to require industry to pay its pollution costs should be neutral in the medium term. In the short term there may be some adjustment problems but these can be assisted with short term compensatory subsidies, a use of subsidy which is permitted under the Polluter-Pays Principle.

Chapter V

The International Dimension

Applying economic instruments in environmental protection bears an international dimension in two respects: First, economic instruments, as any other policy instrument, affect producers and consumers and thus have an impact on international trade. Second, economic instruments could be used to cope with international and global environmental problems.

5.1   The Trade issue

i)   *Background*

It is often asserted that environmental policies should not cause significant distortion in international trade. However, the problem is how to define a trade distortion. From a purely conceptual point of view, international trade is not distorted when trade flows are "naturally" oriented according to the comparative advantages of the different trading partners. Prices should reflect the true productive capabilities of the country including the full social and environmental costs involved in production activities. This is indeed the aim of the Polluter-Pays Principle. If a country has poor hydrological resources and must consequently impose very strict water-quality standards this comparative disadvantage must not be hidden by public assistance to polluters. If, on the other hand, this country benefits from important free space resources it should take full advantage of it by, for instance, imposing relatively less stringent standards for air pollution if it can be adequately dispersed over the available free space.

However this definition of trade distortion refers to a hypothetical situation of perfect competition, and it is now recognised that trade today is much more likely to take place under conditions of imperfect competition, scale economies and product differentiation. Trade distortions are produced by a variety of types of measures:

trade policy measures (such as tariffs, quantitative controls, export subsidies, etc.) as well as more general government policy actions affecting the economic and social climate (in such fields as investment, anti-trust, domestic subsidies, etc.). The role of environment measures in the overall picture of trade distortions may or may not be significant.

In these circumstances, the issue is less one of avoiding distortions than of ensuring that countries pursue environmental policy objectives in the least trade-distorting-way --preferably in ways that reduce the overall level of international distortion. In this perspective, the absence of environmental policy may itself be seen as a cause of trade distortion, since prices would not fully reflect the social costs which it is broadly considered necessary to accept. Similarly, when producers are required to internalise environmental costs, this may be seen as a means for eliminating distortions. Other policies, such as government assistance to polluters, would tend to maintain a distorted international competitive situation.

Hence, as a general rule, environmental policies in different countries have to be based on a common cost-allocation principle, (i.e. the Polluter-Pays Principle), to prevent occurrence of new trade distortions. Taking due account of diversities between different countries and regions is, in fact, an important condition for efficient environmental management, both at a national and an international level, since each policy must fit as much as possible into the environmental conditions, social preferences, and economic structures prevailing in each country. This diversity of situations calls for a diversity of policy instruments (all based on the Polluter-Pays Principle), whether in the form of pollution standards or charges. Both types of instruments have to be adapted to the national, regional or local environmental conditions in order to ensure an efficient achievement of quality objectives.

Thus, the international harmonization of environmental policy instruments would be required essentially in two types of situations: 1) to prevent the introduction of deliberate or unintentional trade distortions 2) when countries or a group of countries estimate that some form of harmonization or concerted action is required to achieve specific objectives and priorities (such as the removal of trade barriers within the European Single Market). For instance, international harmonisation can be seen as giving business a more predictable perspective on which to plan ahead; it might also help in obtaining wider country participation in common environmental action (on the understanding that some flexibility of implementation would be allowed within harmonised global objectives and/or procedures); finally, if exceptions to normal trading principles are required to support environmental policies, harmonisation of these policies might help obtaining easier and wider acceptance of GATT waivers, since they would not lead to a free for all situation.

It should be noted that the meaning of international "harmonization" is rather vague and seems to convey a variety of meanings. "Harmonization" is taken here as a **generic term** encompassing several forms of concerted action such as: 1) uniformisation of policies (e.g. uniform taxes and standards); 2) agreement on common policy instruments (e.g. charges) but leaving freedom to each country to adapt its implementation and form 3) agreement on common principles (e.g. the Polluter-Pays Principle). Therefore the term "coordination" is sometimes preferred to "harmonisation".

In the specific case of economic instrument, while a strict uniformisation of economic instruments may not be necessary (disregarding for the moment global and transfrontier pollution problems), a degree of international co-operation would be useful in specific situations which ought to be assessed, according to the type of economic instrument and the type of issue at stake. To this end a differentiation must be made between economic instrument applicable to **domestic** environmental issues and those designed to cope with **international** issues.

ii) *Types of economic instruments*

When economic instruments are implemented to cope with national or regional environmental problems **with no international spillovers**, four types of economic instruments should be differentiated:

Emission charges

Emission charges imposed on industry should be devised so as to cope with national and regional pollution problems, i.e. their basis should be adapted to local pollution issues and their rates should vary to ensure an efficient achievement of objectives. For instance, charges on effluent discharge in a river could be modulated according to the water quality, assimilative capacity and types of dischargers on various stretches of the river. Consequently, effluent charges should be allowed to differ across countries.

Concerted action, however, may be required if it is estimated that trade and other benefits accruing from harmonized or uniform charging systems outweigh efficiency losses due to non adaptation of charges to local environmental and socio-economic situations.

Product charges

Taxing products containing pollutants or causing pollution at the production consumption or disposal stage is an already widespread and quickly developing practice. A distinction must be drawn between two cases:

-- If the tax on the polluting product is levied at the **consumption or retail level**, no trade distortions will ensue because domestic and foreign producers are in the same competitive situation. Neither differing rates nor differing tax basis will cause market segmentation.

-- However, taxing products at the **production stage**, can result in both trade and environmental distortions because 1) exported products would suffer a competitive disadvantage if the country of destination does not apply similar charges to its domestic products and 2) export prices, including the "environmental tax" of the exporting country, will not necessarily represent the environmental endowment of the importing country. In this case international harmonization of taxes may be required.

Deposit-refund systems

Although deposit refund systems operate as purely domestic instruments and apply to end users exclusively, international trade issues may arise, for example, when products are subject to import restrictions because their packaging do not fit into domestic deposit-refund schemes.

Marketable permits

When applied to domestic problems, the main objective of marketable permits is to implement the most cost-effective solution to achieve or maintain an ambient quality objective within a given area. It should not introduce trade distortion and there are no reason for an international harmonization when no transfrontier or global pollution issues are at stake. If initial permits are granted freely to existing polluters ("grandfathering") new entrants who have to purchase permits, suffer a competitive disadvantage. This, however, applies both to domestic and foreign competitors.

5.2   Applying economic instruments to global environmental problems

i)   *Background*

Global environmental issues arise where there is global environmental interdependence -- that is, where all countries have a stake in the issue and where the actions of any one country affect the welfare of all others. Examples include global warming, stratospheric ozone depletion, the extinction of species and the preservation of unique environments like the Antarctic. Local environmental problems like smog are pervasive around the globe but the damage they cause is almost exclusively felt by people living in the vicinity of the pollution. Other environmental problems like acid rain and pollution of the Great Lakes or Mediterranean involve interdependence but on a more limited scale.

There are two types of global environmental problems. **Reciprocal externalities** arise when every country contributes directly to the environmental problem. All countries influence the carbon cycle and hence all affect the concentration of greenhouse gases in the atmosphere directly. Similarly, all countries use products that contain, or were made from, CFC's, and hence all contribute directly to the depletion of stratospheric ozone.

Some global environmental problems involve **unidirectional externalities**. All countries may be harmed by tropical deforestation both because of the loss of unique natural environments and because of the reduction in the stock of biological diversity. Yet according to international law, ownership of these resources belongs to the tropical countries, and only they can determine how these resources are used. Likewise, all countries may suffer from the excesses of commercial whaling or mineral exploitation in the Antarctic, but only a few countries are in a position to exploit these resources.

Resolution of global environmental problems of either type is made difficult by the built-in incentives for "free riding" behaviour. For reciprocal externalities, if any country reduces its rate of pollution, all others will benefit while only the one country will bear the cost. Each country will ignore the benefit its pollution control confers on others, and hence pollute too much. Exactly the same incentives exist for unidirectional externalities. The important difference between the two types of problem is that for reciprocal externalities the actions of one country can be reciprocated by others. If one uncooperative country pollutes more, others can pollute more, too, to punish the offender. Hence, co-operation of a kind could potentially be countenanced.

For unidirectional externalities, no such possibility exists. If a tropical country destroys its forests, there is no way non-tropical countries can reciprocate unless the "game" is enlarged to include other issues like development assistance and trade. However, the other nations that have a stake in what the tropical countries do can provide these countries with incentives to protect their rain forests. Transfers can help in the management of reciprocal externalities but they are not necessary for making partial progress. The Montreal Protocol on Substances that Deplete the Ozone Layer, for example, commits a substantial number of countries to undertake significant levels of pollution control without transfers, although transfers may be necessary to induce other countries to sign the Protocol. If any progress is to be made in correcting unidirectional externalities, however, transfers are vital. Transfers need not be monetary; they may, for example, involve access to abatement technology.

Resolution of both types of problem seems to demand formal international agreement, and many such agreements already exist (11). Global environmental problems have not previously been managed using economic instruments. However, progress in negotiating agreements seems to be quickening, and interest in using economic instruments for implementing such agreements is growing. Economic instruments could be employed at the national level as a means of effectively implementing the requirements of an international agreement, or they could be used at the international level. Agreements usually leave it to the signatories themselves to decide how to implement a national obligation. However, if instruments were to be used at the international level, special provisions for doing so would have to be included in the agreement itself (or in amendments to the agreement).

ii) *Purpose and framework*

As in other areas, economic instruments may serve the purpose of providing incentives for, or financing investments in, environmental protection. Intergovernmental transfers, for example, may be financed by charges.

Unlike most other environmental issues, global issues as such will often not already be subject to direct regulation (although sources contributing to the problem may be regulated). When economic incentives are grafted onto an inherited structure of direct regulation, the principal goal is for the reforms to improve the efficiency of the original regulations. However, it is likely that in many cases environmental regulation would have been even more efficient had economic instruments been incorporated from the start. Since the slate for regulating global environmental problems is pretty clean, it is possible that economic instruments might be able to achieve a great deal if employed initially. However, in some cases it could still be desirable for economic instruments to be used as a complement to direct regulations.

iii)   *Type of economic instruments*

Emission charges

Charges intended to protect the environment must be imposed on emissions themselves since it is emissions that cause environmental damage. However, charging on the basis of emissions is not always easy, not least because emissions can be difficult to monitor. For many global environmental problems it turns out that emissions can be related directly to products. For these cases, an emission charge can be identical to a product charge or a deposit refund scheme.

Product charges

As a practical matter, carbon dioxide emissions cannot be removed by any currently available end-of-pipe treatment. Hence, emissions are perfectly correlated with the carbon content of the fuels being burned. A charge on carbon will therefore be identical to an emission charge on carbon dioxide. The charge on carbon can be translated into a product charge on fossil fuels given information about the carbon content of these fuels.

The aim of any policy intending to address the potential for global warming must be to reduce the concentration of greenhouse gases in the atmosphere and take actions that will reduce the damage that might be caused. A policy on global warming needs to be comprehensive if it is to address this problem in an efficient manner. This means that policy should seek to reduce the emission of **all** greenehouse gases. It also means that policy should encourage activities that enhance the ability of the environment to **absorb** greenhouse gases. Deforestation increases emissions while reforestation reduces emissions. If deforestation were subject to a charge, reforestation would need to be subject to a negative charge, or a subsidy.

Deposit-refund systems

Deposit-refund systems are usually applied to products. However, where products can be correlated perfectly with emissions, deposit-refund systems can have the same effect as an emission charge system; For example, sources of carbon dioxide emissions could be required to pay a deposit on emissions which would be refunded if and only if the sources invested in sink enhancement.

In the case of the hard CFCs listed under the Montreal Protocol, it is sometimes suggested that these could be regulated by requiring that producers and importers pay a deposit on their traded volumes and receive a refund for the amounts they recycle. Such a policy would, however, be inefficient; it would encourage too much recycling. If producers pay a charge for their production and imported volumes, then the existing stock of these substances automatically increases in value. Producers can supply their customers either by manufacturing or importing additional CFCs (or hard CFC-substitutes), or by recycling CFCs from the existing stock If suppliers manufacture or import CFCs, they must pay the charge. If they recycle CFCs they avoid having to pay the charge. Hence, no additional incentive is required to induce recycling. A refund can be required on CFCs that are safely destroyed or exported.

Marketable permits

As a form of quantity regulation, marketable permits can be particularly effective at meeting a quantitative emission reduction goal. However, trading, like charging, is complicated when emissions are difficult to monitor. For the cases of carbon dioxide and substances that deplete the ozone layer, however, emissions can be perfectly correlated with products, and this makes regulation by marketable permits simpler to implement.

Importantly, provisions in the Montreal Protocol allow (implicitly) for limited trading in production and consumption allowances for the controlled substances. According to the Protocol, one country can produce somewhat more of the conrolled substances provided another country agrees to produce somewhat less and the production restrictions are met **in total** for the two parties (at least one of these parties must have produced no more than 25 kilotonnes of the controlled substances in 1986). Consumption trades are also permitted within "regional economic integration organisations" like the European Community on an unlimited basis provided the total combined consumption target for the organisation is not exceeded.

Emission offsets

An alternative approach could be used to regulate pollutants like carbon dioxide and CFCs. Suppose the goal is to hold emissions constant. Then existing emission sources could be allowed to increase emissions, and new sources could be allowed to emit carbon dioxide, provided they can get some other source to reduce emissions by an equivalent amount. Alternatively, increases in emissions could be offset by investments which increase the environment's ability to absorb the pollutant. The principal attraction of an offset policy is that existing polluters are not made any worse off compared to their current situation.

iv)   *Field of operation*

Pollutants/processes/products

For global pollution problems, economic instruments should be targeted at controlling emissions. For some problems -- namely, carbon dioxide emissions and emissions of controlled substances subject to the Montreal Protocol (CFD-11, -12,- 113, -114, and -115; and halon-1211,-1301, and -2402) -- emissions are highly correlated with products. As noted earlier, this makes the use of economic instruments very attractive.

In regulating emissions, it is important that policy consider the implications for environmental quality. Many CFC compounds deplete stratospheric ozone. Rather than control each compound separately, policy should seek a more comprehensive approach. Under the Montreal Protocol, weights are attached to each of the listed substances according to their ozone depleting potential. As a consequence, the listed substances are regulated as a goup. This approach is far more efficient than one which regulated each substance separately (12).

A similar approach should be employed for controlling greenhouse gases. The greenhouse gases include not just carbon dioxide but CFCs and halons (the same substances that deplete stratospheric ozone), methane, nitrous oxide, and tropospheric ozone. Other pollutants, like carbon monoxide, are not greenhouse gases **per se** but react in the atmosphere to form carbon dioxide. Since all of the these emissions contribute to potential global climate change, none should be excluded from proposed regulations. In principle, a "global warming potential" weight could be applied to each pollutant. This weight would reflect the pollutant's potential for "radiative forcing" -- that is, the efficiency with which the gas absorbs thermal radiation -- as well as the likely lifetime of a unit of emission in the atmosphere.

Target groups

The target groups will vary from problem to problem. In the OECD countries, all sectors emit CFCs. Yet only a few firms supply these gases. For

95

example, in the United States -- the largest producer and consumer of hard CFCs -- only 16 firms produce and/or consume (that is, import or export) substances controlled under the Montreal Protocol. In the United Kingdom, only two companies produce CFCs. Charges can be imposed at the point of consumption or production. For practical reasons, marketable permits would have to aply to producers and importers only.

Greenhouse gases are also emitted by every sector in the economy. Carbon dioxide emissions could be controlled by marketable permits allocated to producers. However, there are alternatives that may appear more attractive. One would be a carbon charge on fossil fuels. Another would be a combined marketable permits/emission charge scheme. Large emission sources like electricity producers could be allocated marketable permits while small sources like households could be subject to a carbon charge (for example, on gasoline and home heating fuels). Either way, provisions must be included which encourage the enhancement of carbon "sinks".

Other greenhouse gases also result from fossil fuel combustion -- namely tropospheric ozone, nitrous oxide, and carbon monoxide. Nitrous oxide is also emitted by the agricultural sector. Methane is emitted by agriculture, landfills and from natural gas deposits and transmission pipelines.

v)   *Mode of operation: formulae and implementation*

Formulae

      Where charges are used to raise revenue, the size of the charge needed to raise a particular amount of money can be computed using information on the price-responsiveness of the demand for the product that is subject to the charge; A similar approach can be used to determine the effectiveness of an incentive charge.

      A carbon charge could be imposed as a product charge on fossil fuels using information on the carbon content of these fuels. Similarly, a charge on CFCs and halons would need to be weighted by the ozone depleting potential of the controlled substances. The emission reductions that would be achieved by any charge could be predicted using information about the responsiveness of product demands to changes in relative prices. Consideration would have to be given to how producers will respond to the charge, and whether there might be strong second order effects; For example, a very large carbon charge -- say, on the border of the OPEC price increases of the 1970s -- imposed rapidly could conceivably reduce the rate of economic growth, which would in turn affect fuel demands. A reform of tax/benefit policy generally might mean offsetting the increase in revenue arising from the carbon charge with a reduction in the rate of distortionary taxes like income taxes or taxes on savings (13). If these distortionary taxes were lowered to offset the revenues obtained by the carbon charge, there would be macroeconomic consequences that would influence the effect the charge would have on emission reduction.

A negative charge (or refund) on activities that create carbon sinks or safely destroy CFCs and halons would have to be consistent with the positive charge (or deposit) on emissions. For both cases, the negative charge on activities that reduce the concentration of the pollutant by one unit should equal the positive charge on activities that increase concentration by one unit.

Transfers of permits between polluters should also reflect the relative importance f the pollutnt in achieving the environmental quality objective or total emission reduction goal. Trades in CFC quotas, for example, should be adjusted for the ozone depleting potential of the CFCs.

Competence

Economic instruments could form part of an international agreement, or the agreement could state the obligations of signatories and leave it to these countries to decide how to meet their obligations. In either case, a secretariat of some kind would be needed to monitor compliance. The role played by the Secretariat could vary substantially. For example, charges might be collected and distributed by the Secretariat itself, or these tasks could be performed entirely by national governments. For unidirectional externalities, it would seem that transfers would have to be organised by the Secretariat, as indeed is the case with the World Heritage Convention. For reciprocal externalities, either option could prove effective.

Whichever approach is taken, instruments should be applied as widely as possible. This means that national obligations should be implemented using economic instruments where appropriate, and that international agreements should allow their use on an international basis. For example, an agreement which sets quantitative emission reductions for individual countries should allow these countries to trade their reduction responsibilities so as to achieve the ultimate environmental goal at the lowest possible cost.

Calculation

Calculation of charges and terms for trading for carbon dioxide emissions and CFs poses no great problem because the products themselves form the basis for assessment. In other cases, calculation can be difficult. For example, a refund or negative charge on reforestation would ideally be based on the reduction in the atmospheric concentration of carbon dioxide resulting from the activity. As a practical matter, however, the refund or negative charge would probably have to be based on activities that are easily observable. If the assessment were based on the number of trees planted, there may be an incentive for an excessive number of trees to be planted on any given plot of land, while if the assessment were based on the area that is reforested, there may be an incentive for too few trees to be planted per unit of land area. But of course these problems would also plague any direct regulation for reforestation. What is needed is a simple formula that strikes the best compromise between efficiency and practicality. For reforestation, a per hectare charge/refund adjusted for the number of trees per hectare might be most appropriate.

Invoice

As noted earlier, for some global pollutants like carbon dioxide and CFCs, emissions correlate very well with products. One of the advantages of this correlation is in invoicing polluters for emission charges. In the case of carbon dioxide, taxes on fuels already exist in most countries. A simple readjustment in the basis for taxation would be required, but invoicing would demand no additional resources. This is a major attraction of the carbon charge.

Other products may not already be taxed separately. However, for products like CFCs, charges would be easily invoiced because production is simple to monitor and only a few companies produce these substances. Taxing consumers of these products would be much more difficult administratively.

Manpower and costs

The full costs of implementation must be reflected in the design of economic incentives for environmental protection. Trading emission allowances may entail large transactions costs, both for the firms engaging in trades and the agency supervising the trading. Institutions like brokerage houses might emerge to reduce these costs, but regulations should seek to keep transactions costs low.

Chapter VI

Summary: Check List of Relevant Points

DEFINITION

Charges on the discharge of pollutants into air, water or soil, based on quantity and quality of pollutant.

SPECIFIC PURPOSE AND ADVANTAGES

- Savings in compliance costs.
- Potential incentive effect.
- Revenue raising.
- Flexibility.

APPROPRIATE CIRCUMSTANCES

- Mainly stationary sources.
- Variation in marginal abatement cost between polluters.
- Feasibility and reasonable cost of monitoring emissions.
- Potential for polluters to reduce emission and change behaviour.
- Potential for technical innovation.

RELEVANCE TO ENVIRONMENTAL MEDIA/ISSUES

Water	-	<u>High</u>
		Examples: Surface water charges in France, Germany, The Netherlands.
Air	-	<u>Medium</u>, due to monitoring difficulties.
		Examples: Charges on NO_x emissions in Sweden.
Waste	-	<u>Low</u>, due to complexity of waste stream. Only for stationary sources; user charges most appropriate.
		Examples: Hazardous waste tax and feedstock charge in the United States. Surplus manure charge in the Netherlands.

Cont'd

Check List of Relevant Points: **EMISSION CHARGES**

Noise   -   <u>High</u> for aircraft. <u>Low</u> for other vehicles.
             Examples: Aircraft noise charges in the Netherlands and Switzerland.

ISSUES

- Complexity and administrative cost of detailed charges based on all relevant pollutants.
- Distributive effects need to be carefully assessed.
- In case of earmarking revenue, need for a coherent allocation system.

DEFINITION

Charges levied on products that are harmful to the environment when used in production processes, consumed or disposed of.

SPECIFIC PURPOSE AND ADVANTAGES

- Reduce use of products and/or induce product substitution.
- Incentive effect.
- Revenue raising.
- In some cases, useful proxy for emission charges.
- Applicable to diffuse and mobile sources.
- Ease of implementation.
- Flexibility.

APPROPRIATE CIRCUMSTANCES

- Products used in large quantities or volumes.
- Products easily identifiable.
- High demand elasticity.
- Substitution possibilities.
- Need to control diffuse sources.
- Possibility to use existing administrtive and fiscal channels.

RELEVANCE TO ENVIRONMENTAL MEDIA/ISSUES

Water - <u>Medium</u>. For products likely to pollute surface or groundwater.
Examples: Charges on fertilizers and pesticides in Norway and Sweden; charges on lubricant oils in Finland and Germany.

Check List of Relevant Points: PRODUCT CHARGES

Air	-	High, in particular for fuels.
		Examples: Charges on sulphur content of fuels in France; charges on motor-vehicle fuels in Finland and Sweden; differential taxes on leaded and unleaded gasoline (France, Germany, Norway, United Kingdom etc.).
Waste	-	High. For products that need to be recycled or safely disposed of.
		Examples: Charges on non-returnable beverage containers in Finland, on plastic bags in Italy, on lubricating oils in France, Germany etc.
Noise	-	Medium. For motor-vehicles according to noise emission levels.
		Examples: None.

ISSUES

- Not applicable to highly toxic products (a ban is preferable).
- Low demand elasticities and substitution possibilities for certain products (e.g., gasoline).
- Trade and competitiveness implications.
- Possible administrative problems.

Check List of Relevant Points: DEPOSIT-REFUND SYSTEMS

DEFINITION

Deposit [charge] levied on a potentially polluting product, to be refunded when the product is returned to storage, treatment or recycling point.

SPECIFIC PURPOSE AND ADVANTAGES

- Induce safe disposal, reuse or recycling of products.
- Effectiveness in reducing waste stream volume.
- Flexibility.
- Easy application if geared on existing distribution systems.

APPROPRIATE CIRCUMSTANCES

- Serious environmental problems attached to disposal.
- Recycling and reuse feasible and profitable (market for recycled material).
- Co-operative behaviour of producers, retailers and users.
- Low administrative cost.

RELEVANCE TO ENVIRONMENTAL MEDIA/ISSUES

Water - <u>Low.</u> Could be applied to containers of water pollutants such as pesticides or products (mercury and cadmium in batteries).
Examples: None but under consideration for batteries in a few countries.

Air - <u>Medium.</u> For products containing potentially air pollutants (e.g., CFC's in refrigerators) or containers which pollute air while burned (plastics).
Examples: None but under consideration for plastic containers.

104

Check List of Relevant Points: DEPOSIT-REFUND SYSTEMS

Waste	-	<u>High</u>.
	Examples:	Car bulks in Norway and Sweden, beverage containers in many countries.
Noise	-	<u>Nil</u>.

ISSUES

- Possible ill-adaptation of distribution systems.
- Balance between deposit level and product or waste price.
- Risk of evasion (illegal dumping).
- Possible trade implications.

DEFINITION

Environmental quotas, allowances or ceiling on emission levels that, once initially allocated by the appropriate authority, can be traded subject to a set of prescribed rules.

SPECIFIC PURPOSE AND ADVANTAGES

- Savings in compliance cost.
- Compatibility between economic-industrial growth in a given area and environmental protection.
- Flexibility.

APPROPRIATE CIRCUMSTANCES

- Differences in marginal compliance costs between regulated target groups.
- Maximum ambient pollutant concentrations are fixed and/or reached.
- Number of sources involved, large enough to establish a well functioning market.
- More easily applicable to fixed sources.
- Potential for technical innovation.
- Environmental impact is independent of sources' locations.
- Environmental impact loosely connected to time of pollutants release.
- Elaborated implementation structure feasible and not too costly.

RELEVANCE TO ENVIRONMENTAL MEDIA/ISSUES

Water - Low, because environmental impact of discharge highly dependent on source location and period of the year.
Examples: A few cases in the United States.

Check List of Relevant Points: MARKETABLE PERMITS

Air - <u>High</u>
Examples: United States' bubbles and offset programmes, lead in gasoline, can coating facilities.

Waste - <u>Low</u>, because environmental impact highly dependent on location of waste.
Examples: None but projects in the United States.

Noise - <u>Low</u>, because noise impact dependent of source location. May be envisaged for aircraft.
Examples: None.

ISSUES

- Limited applicability to more than one pollutant simultaneously, unless some "equivalence index" can be developed.
- Possible negative local environmental impact if the effect of emissions is sensitive to the location of emissions' sources, especially when toxic substances are involved.
- Initial allocation of permits/allowances, needs careful consideration and implementation.
- Initial goals (baselines) also need precise and careful definition.
- Need to define carefully geographical scope of tradings.
- Implementation and enforcement rules and procedures may be complex.
- High transaction cost.

Notes and References

(1)   "Guiding Principles Concerning International Economic Aspects of Environmental Politics" (Recommendation adopted by the OECD Council on 26th May, 1972) C(72)128

       "The Implementation of the Polluter-Pays Principle" (Recommendation adopted by the OECD Council on 14th November, 1974) C(74)223

(2)   OECD (1980), *Pollution Charges in Practice,* Paris.

(3)   A number of OECD Recommendations advocate the use of economic instruments, for example:

       "Water Management Policies and Instruments" (Recommendation adopted on 5th April,1978) C(78)4(Final)

       "Water Resource Management Policies: Integration, Demand Management, and Groundwater Protection" (Recommendation adopted by the Council at its 704th Session on 31st March, 1989) C(89)12(Final)

       "Noise Abatement Policies" (Recommendation adopted by the Council on 3rd July, 1978) C(78)(Final)

       Recommendation on the Application of the Polluter-Pays Principle to Accidental Pollution (adopted by the Council on 7th July, 1989 at its 712th Session) C(89)88(Final)

       "A Comprehensive Waste Management Policy" (Recommendation by the OECD Council on 28th September, 1976) C(76)155(Final)

       "The Re-Use and Recycling of Beverage Containers" (Recommendation adopted on 3rd February, 1978) C(78)8(Final)

(4)   OECD (1989), *Economic Instruments for Environmental Protection*, Paris.

(5)   Communiqué of the OECD Council, C(89)99 - G7 Summit of the Arch, 14th-16th July, 1989, Economic Declaration

(6)   OECD (1989), *Environmental Policy Benefits: Monetary Valuation*, Paris.

(7)   OECD (1991), *Market and Intervention Failures in Transport Policy*, Paris.

(8)   Some EFTA-countries have already implemented such charges on mineral fertilizers and pesticides. The Netherlands have introduced a charge on feedstuffs. Up to now, however, the main purpose is to raise funds, and charge rates are low. Nevertheless, there seems to be at least some adjustment in intensities.

(9)   Based on model calculations, many studies on input charges conclude that due to very low price elasticities, charge rates would have to be very high. Such models, however, tend to underestimate the real scope for adjustment. Furthermore, they often start from the assumption that all farms already produce close to the economic optimum. They also often neglect the various options for substitution and the potentials for induced technological innovations. Recent experience with relatively modest charges on nitrogen fertilizer suggests that even at a low rate, considerable adjustments can be achieved.

(10)   See OECD, "Improving the Enforcement of Environmental Policy", Environment Monograph n° 8, Paris, 1987

(11)   Co-operation in protection the ozone layer is codified in the Vienna Convention for the Protection of the Ozone Layer and the associated Montreal Protocol. The latter agreement includes statutory limits on the production and consumption of CFCs. Preservation of biological diversity and unique natural environments can, to some extent, be handled by the Convention Concerning the Protection of the World Cultural and Natural Heritage, which facilitates small transfers to countries bearing the costs of preserving unique environments of global significance. Use of the Antartic resources is co-ordinated by the Antartic Treaty. Informal negotiations on an international agreement on global warming are already underway.

(12)   For example, the Montreal Protocol assigns a weight of 1.0 to CFC-11 and a weight of 0.8 to CFC-113. Since the production restrictions in the Protocol apply to the group of listed substances, producing countries can

comply with the Protocol by reducing production of some coumpounds by more than others. It is even possible for production of one compound to increase provided production of others falls by a sufficient amount. This is an efficient means of regulating harmful emissions, although it should be mentioned that the Protocol assigns a weight of zero (effectively) to other substances that deplete the ozone layer and yet are not included in the agreement.

(13)   An income tax is distortionary because it creates disincentives to work: people find it more attractive to substitute untaxed leisure for income producing activities. A savings tax is distortionary because it provides an incentive for people to substitute consumption now for consumption later, and hence lowers the rate of saving.

Part II

Recommendation of the Council on
the Use of Economic Instruments in Environmental Policy

(adopted by the Council at its 750th Session on 31st January 1991)

THE COUNCIL,

Having regard to Article 5b) of the Convention on the Organisation for Economic Co- Operation and Development of 14th December 1960;

Having regard to the Recommendation of the Council of 26th May 1972 on Guiding Principles Concerning International Economic Aspects of Environmental Policies [C(72)128];

Having Regard to the Recommendation of the Council of 14th November 1974 on the Implementation of the Polluter-Pays Principle [C(74)223];

Having Regard to the Recommendation of the Council of 7th July 1989 on the Application of the Polluter-Pays Principle to Accidental Pollution [C(89)88(Final);

Having Regard to the Council's Acts which recommend the use of economic instruments in various policy fields, namely: the Recommendation of the Council of 28th September 1976 on a Comprehensive Waste Management Policy [C(76)155(Final); the Recommendation of the Council of 5th April 1978 on Water Management Policies and Instruments [C(78)4(Final)]; the Recommendation of the Council of 3rd February 1978 on the Re-Use and Recycling of Beverage Containers [C(78)8(Final)]; the Recommendation of the Council of 3rd July 1978 on Noise Abatement Policies [C(78)73(Final)]; the Recommendation of the Council of 20th June 1985 on Strenghening Noise Abatement Policies [C(85)103]; the Recommendation of the Council of 31st March 1989 on Water Resource Management Policies: Integration, Demand Management, and Groundwater Protection [C(89)12(Final)];

Having regard to the Declaration on "Environment: Resources for the Future" adopted by Member Governments during the meeting of the Environment Committee at Ministerial level on 20th June 1985 which states that Member countries will "Seek to introduce more flexibility, efficiency and cost-effectiveness in the design and enforcement of pollution control measures in particular through a consistent application of the Polluter-Pays Principle and a more effective use of economic instruments in conjunction with regulations;"

Having regard to the OECD Council Ministerial Communiqué of 31st May 1990, which states that the OECD should design "Guidelines for the use of economic instruments and of market mechanisms to achieve environmental goals";

Having regard to the Ministerial Declaration of the Second World Climate Conference of 7th November 1990, which states: "the adoption of any form of economic or regulatory measures should require careful and substantive analyses. We recommend that relevant policies make use of economic instruments appropriate to each country's socio- economic conditions in conjunction with a balanced mix of regulatory approaches."

Considering that a sustainable and economically efficient management of environmental resources requires, inter alia, the internalisation of pollution prevention, control and damage costs;

Considering that such internalisation can be enhanced by a consistent use of market mechanisms, in particular those economic instruments defined in the Annex to this Recommendation;

I   RECOMMENDS that Member countries:

   i)   make a greater and more consistent use of economic instruments as a complement or a substitute to other policy instruments such as regulations, taking into account national socio-economic conditions;

   ii)   work towards improving the allocation and efficient use of natural and environmental resources by means of economic instruments so as to better reflect the social cost of using these resources;

   iii) make effort to reach further agreement at international level on the use of environmental policy instruments with respect to solving regional or global environmental problems as well as ensuring sustainable development;

iv)   develop better modelling, forecasting and monitoring techniques to provide information on environmental consequences of alternative policy actions and their economic effects;

v)   integrate environmental and economic decision-making in sectoral policies in order to avoid adverse effects on environmental resources, e.g. as could be the case for price-support mechanisms in sectors such as energy, agriculture and transport.

II   RECOMMENDS that, when using economic instruments, Member countries take into account the Guidelines and considerations set out in the Annex hereto, which is an integral part of this Recommendation.

III   INSTRUCTS the Environment Committee and other relevant bodies of the Organisation (in particular, the Economic Policy Committee):

i)   to support Member countries' efforts in applying economic instruments through an exchange of information concerning, in particular design or choice of economic instruments, taxation reforms, modelling, forecasting and monitoring techniques, institutional arrangements, regulatory reform and deregulation, removal of environmentally damaging sectoral subsidies in order to:

-- enhance international co-ordination of environmental policies with respect to global and regional environmental problems;

-- develop its work on economic instruments in order to assist Member States in the choice of the most cost effective policy instruments and to provide information regarding their effectiveness in achieving specific environmental objectives.

ii)   to review the actions taken by Member countries pursuant to this Recommendation within the three years following the adoption of this Recommendation.

ANNEX

Guidelines and Considerations for the Use of Economic Instruments in Environmental Policy*

I TYPES OF ECONOMIC INSTRUMENTS TO WHICH THE GUIDELINES APPLY

1. Economic instruments have the potential to be applied to a wide range of environmental and natural resources issues. The present guidelines deal with the use of economic instruments defined hereunder. In addition, there are other types of economic instruments such as enforcement incentives, fines, non-compliance fees, administrative charges, performance bonds, damage compensation etc. which may have a role in environmental policy but are not considered here. Furthermore, the guidelines focus primarily on pollution issues although economic instruments also have considerable potential for application in the form of resource pricing.

Charges and taxes

2. Emission charges or taxes are payments on the emission of pollutants into air or water or onto or into soil and on the generation of noise. Emission charges or taxes are calculated on the basis of the quantity and type of pollutant discharged.

3. User charges or taxes are payments for the costs of collective treatment of effluent or waste.

---

* The Guidelines set out in this Annex are based on the review of Member countries' experience in using economic instruments [see OECD, Economic Instruments for Environmental Protection, Paris, 1989] and on detailed Guidelines prepared by an OECD "Task Force on Economic Instruments" and by the OECD Group of Economic Experts.

4.   Product charges or taxes are levied on products that are harmful to the environment when used in production processes, consumed or disposed of. Product charges or taxes can act as a substitute for emission charges or taxes when charging directly for emissions is not feasible. They may be applied to raw materials, intermediate or final (consumer) products. Product tax differentiation may be designed for the same purpose.

Marketable Permits

5.   Marketable permits are quotas, allowances or ceilings on pollution emission levels of specified polluters that, once allocated by the appropriate authority, can be traded subject to a set of prescribed rules. Hence, marketable permits provide an incentive for dischargers releasing less pollution than their limits allow, to trade the differences between actual discharges and allowable discharges to other dischargers which then have the right to release more than allowed by initial limits. Under different approaches, these trades can take place within a plant, within a firm, among different firms, or possibly between countries. The objective is to reach the overall pollution ceiling with maximum efficiency. Equally, marketable permits can be used as a device to encourage efficient use of natural resources such as scarce water supplies.

Deposit-refund Systems

6.   With deposit-refund systems, a deposit is paid on the acquisition of potentially polluting products. When pollution is avoided by returning the products or their residuals, a refund follows.

Financial Assistance

7.   Various forms of financial assistance can be granted to polluters as help and/or as an inducement to abate their polluting emissions. As a general rule, financial assistance is incompatible with the Polluter-Pays-Principle, except in a few specific cases, for example, when in compliance with the exceptions to the Polluter-Pays-Principle as defined in the two Council Recommendations [C(72)128 and C(74)223] or when applied in the framework of appropriately designed redistributive charging systems.

There may also be circumstances where payments can be made to reinforce other measures designed to achieve appropriate natural resource use.

II   CRITERIA FOR CHOICE OF INSTRUMENTS

8.   Economic instruments constitute one category amongst others of instruments designed to achieve environmental goals.   They can be used as a substitute or as a complement to other policy instruments such as regulations and co-operative agreements with industry.   In some instances, for economic and administrative reasons, direct regulation and control are appropriate when, for example, it is imperative that the emission of certain toxic pollutants or the use of hazardous products or substances be wholly prohibited.   In other instances, economic instruments can supplement regulations in order to strengthen the enforcement of standards designed to protect public health.

9.   The choice of environmental policy instruments can be made against five sets of criteria:

i)   Environmental effectiveness: The environmental effectiveness of economic instruments is mainly determined by the ability of polluters to react.   The primary objective of economic instruments is to provide a permanent incentive to pollution abatement, technical innovation, and product substitution.

ii)   Economic efficiency: In a broad sense, economic efficiency is achieved by an optimal allocation of resources;   in a limited but more operational sense, it implies that the economic cost of complying with environmental requirements is minimised.

iii)   Equity: Distributive consequences vary according to the types of policy instruments applied.   For example, pollution charges or taxes entail additional payment on the discharge of "residual" pollution; additionally their distributive impact would depend upon how the revenue is used.   Similarly, with marketable permits, the distributional effects will differ according to their initial allocation.

iv)   Administrative feasibility and cost: All types of policy instruments involve implementation and enforcement structures.   This relates in particular to the ease and cost of monitoring discharges and the number of target groups involved and also upon the nature of existing legal and institutional settings.

v) Acceptability: It is of crucial importance that target groups be informed and consulted on the economic instruments imposed on them. In general, the success of any (economic) instrument requires certainty and stability over time with respect to their basic elements.

10. Regarding the choice of specific economic instruments, the following elements should be taken into consideration:

Emission charges or taxes can be given particular consideration for stationary pollution sources and where marginal abatement costs vary across polluters (the wider the variation, the greater the cost-saving potential). Other criteria are: the feasibility of monitoring emission (through direct monitoring or proxy variables), the ability of polluters to react to the charge, the ability of public authorities to develop a consistent framework for charges, the potential for technical innovation.

User charges are relevant when collective disposal and treatment facilities can be operated, e.g. for waste water, industrial and household waste.

Product charges or taxes can be particularly effective when applied to products that are consumed or used in large quantities and in diffuse patterns. Products subject to charges should be readily identifiable.

Deposit-refund systems can be considered for products or substances which can be reused, recycled or which should be returned for destruction. Because deposit refund schemes can be expensive and complicated to operate, it is important that products be easy to identify and to handle and that users and consumers should also be willing to take part in the scheme.

Marketable permit systems offer particular advantages in situations in which: the marginal costs of compliance with a uniform standard vary significantly across the regulated target group; when there is a fixed objective which one wants to achieve at minimum economic cost; the number of sources involved is large enough to establish a well- functioning, competitive market for permits, within a designated geographical area.

III   GUIDELINES FOR IMPLEMENTING ECONOMIC INSTRUMENTS

11.   When considering the adoption of economic instruments, it is important to assess the cost and benefits of all policy alternatives.   In particular, the development, implementation and enforcement of economic instruments should take due consideration of the issues defined hereunder.

Clear Framework and Objectives

12.   First and foremost, the framework and objectives of the economic instrument must be clear. In particular, the following points should be specified: whether the economic instrument operates in combination with or as an alternative to direct regulation; whether it precedes regulations in order to speed up compliance; whether the revenues are used for general purposes or earmarked for specific environmental or other measures. In the case of charges or taxes, the objective of providing incentives should not be confused with the revenue-raising purpose.

Well-defined Field of Operation

13.   The field of operation must be clearly defined. This includes pollutants, processes or products to which economic instruments are applied. Furthermore, information should be available on the target groups in terms of their number, their size, their contribution to the pertinent problem and the way they pollute (point/non-point sources, mobile/stationary sources), their financial abilities, the way they are organised and likely to react (structure of industry, behaviour of firms, technological characteristics, etc.). However, information requirements should not be excessive.

Simple Mode of Operation

14.   Simplicity and clarity of the mode of operation are of paramount importance and determine to a large extent the administrative efficiency of the economic instrument. This is related to the technicalities of the economic instrument: formulae and calculation of the charge, calculation of emission reduction credits (in case of marketable permits), etc. This also concerns, in terms of new bodies (or in association with existing tax offices), administrative requirements, the way monitoring will take place and the details of invoicing and control. Regarding the "structure" of any economic instrument there should be a fine balance between undue complexity, which makes the instrument hard to apply, and excessive simplicity, which may mean that it is not very efficient. The

amount of information required for the proper operation of any instrument is of decisive importance for its success. Economic instruments aiming at inducing polluters to reduce their emissions are likely to be more complex than those designed purely for revenue-raising purpose. The simplicity or complexity of the mode of operation is mainly related to calculation and invoicing procedures (see below). Further, implementing an excessive number of different economic instruments can lead to confusing price signals and prove to be counterproductive in the long term.

15.   For emission charges or taxes, three ways of calculation exist: 1) monitoring actual discharges, 2) table-based, 3) flat rate. Monitoring might be done either by the responsible administrative body on an annual or more frequent basis, or by the polluter through yearly (or more frequent) returns. Self-monitoring is less costly, but requires a periodic control. Monitoring is advisable for large polluters. Calculation of table-based charge or taxe is a single operation, taking into account general indicators such as the process characteristics of the firm.

16.   For product charges or taxes, rates are fixed. Collection of the revenue can easily fit within existing fiscal channels. Appropriate taxing systems (excise duties, value-added tax) can be efficient structures. Invoicing numerous product charges or taxes at the retailers' level should be avoided. Producers and importers are less numerous, and therefore may be more efficiently administered and more easily controlled.

17.   For marketable permits, complex issues such as the initial allocation of emission quotas (in such a way as to minimise barriers to free entry into the industry), monitoring and the determination of constant or decreasing emission ceilings must be clearly specified. Furthermore, when a net reduction in aggregate discharges is the target, provisions must be made with respect to new entrants in the market.

Acceptability

18.   Acceptability increases by taking into account the following elements:

-- Adequate information disseminated to target groups concerning aspect of the new instrument which may affect them. Important features are the purpose and technicalities of the instrument, financial consequences, time of introduction, possible future adjustments, etc. Timely announcement of new elements is important. Target groups should also be aware of the interrelations between different policy fields.

-- Consultation with target groups should, as far as possible, be conducted concerning application of the instruments. In particular, in order to reduce uncertainty and to ensure a stable policy context, major modifications or plans should be discussed with organizations' representatives or other, diffuse target groups (industry, farmers, consumers etc.). Instruments on the interface of different policy fields should be presented to all relevant parties.

-- Implementation of new economic instruments should be preceded by an appropriate anticipation period and timely announcements. Where appropriate, the implementation should also be progressive, especially for emission charges or taxes and marketable permits in order to enable polluters to adapt and avoid excessively rapid increases in financial burdens (e.g. the rates of pollution charges could be raised progressively to the desired level).

Integration with Sectoral Policies

19.   Economic instruments should be designed to facilitate the integration of environmental policy with other policies, in particular through an appropriate adaptation of various economic sectors' pricing and fiscal structures to conform with environmental goals. Removal and correction of governmental intervention failures such as distorting subsidies in the agricultural field or improper pricing of transport infrastructures, fuels and services, are of utmost importance for a proper integration of environmental policies with sectoral policies. One fundamental objective of economic instruments is to ensure that the prices of goods and services truly reflect the associated environmental costs. This can be achieved only if intervention failures are first removed.

Manpower and Cost of Implementation

20.   Excessive transaction costs should be avoided for enforcement agencies, industry and individuals. The cost effectiveness of implementation and enforcement mechanisms should be carefully assessed. Using existing enforcement channels and invoicing systems could generate substantial cost savings.

Assessment of Economic and Distributive Consequences

21. Several aspects should be distinguished. Firstly, at the micro level, specific (groups of) enterprises may have to face considerable expenditures in a short period of time, which may threaten their continuity. On the other hand, at a more macro level, the instrument concerned will establish efficient solutions in the longer term, if correctly defined. In comparing general long term efficiency and specific short term problems, temporary financial assistance measures for easing transition problems might be adopted, provided that the firms concerned are basically economically sound, even when bearing environmental costs. Applying temporary measures is economically more desirable than granting exemptions to the instrument. The positive economic consequences of economic instruments should be taken into account: for instance, emission tradings allow for ongoing economic growth which would be hampered under strict direct regulation. Incentive charges or taxes (but also direct regulation) may trigger technological innovations, which can create new markets and generate new products.

22. In practice, there are two approaches to the implementation of economic instruments through the fiscal system. One approach is to introduce new product taxes or charges e.g., to impose specific environmental taxes ("eco taxes") on polluting products and substances, such as fuels, pesticides, motor-vehicles, beverage containers. Another approach is to adapt existing tax systems to environmental purposes. This requires, first and foremost, restructuring existing taxes which induce detrimental effects on the environment (e.g., when existing taxes encourage the use of polluting, rather than "clean", products). Economic instruments might generate significant revenue. One possible solution is, when appropriate, given the situation prevailing in each country, to balance the introduction of a new tax with a reduction of existing ones to avoid an additional fiscal burden on the economy. Alternatively, the revenue derived from economic instruments could contribute to reinforcing the budget.

Conformity with General Principles of National and International Trade, Fiscal and Environmental Policy

23. In implementing economic instruments, it is necessary to comply with existing general agreements and principles of environmental policy both at the national and at the international level. One of the most important of these is the "Polluter-Pays"-Principle. Economic instruments, with the exception of financial assistance, are clearly in line with this principle. Principles stemming from trade agreements (e.g., GATT) should also be respected. When introducing economic

124

instruments, unfair competition and international trade distortion must be avoided. Charges or taxes on final products should not discriminate between domestic and imported products.

24. Economic instruments should be in line with existing political, administrative, judicial and fiscal structures. If the introduction of economic instruments does not fit into existing frameworks or requires their modification, the actual implementation will be more complex and difficult. Since, in many instances, economic instruments are of a fiscal character, their compatibility with existing fiscal systems is particularly important. When major tax reforms or deregulation are considered, the possible role of economic instruments within these new frameworks should be examined.

25. When international harmonisation of economic instruments is considered, he different environmental conditions, economic situations and fiscal structures in the countries involved should be given due consideration.

IV. FIELDS OF POSSIBLE APPLICATION OF ECONOMIC INSTRUMENTS*

Water Pollution

26. Water pollution is particularly amenable to emission (effluent) and user charges or taxes as effluent discharge from stationary sources are relatively easy to monitor.

27. Product charges or taxes may be applied in the case of products that will pollute surface or ground water before, during or after consumption. Examples of possible applications relate to detergents, fertilizers and pesticides. If the objective of the product charge or taxe is to discourage consumption, the quantity of the products consumed should be highly sensitive to prices. The availability of cleaner substitutes could considerably increase the success of product charges or differentiated taxes (such as detergents with and without phosphates). Product charges or taxes can also be used as a proxy for emission charges or taxes (e.g. charge on the use of polluting products in production processes).

---

*   For detailed guidelines, see OECD (1991), Guidelines for the Application of Economic Instruments in Environmental Policy, Paris.

28.   Marketable permits could be applied to point sources as well as to combinations of point sources and non-point sources.   In the case of point source/non-point source situations, point sources could obtain additional rights by reducing the pollution burden from non-point sources.

29.   Deposit-refund systems can play an indirect role in water management.   Many potentially polluting substances (for example pesticides) are packed in non-returnable containers.   During disposal of the containers the remnants of these substances are released into the environment and might pollute surface and ground water.   Such remnants can be properly processed when containers are returned to the producer.

30.   Pollutants which are discharged in large quantities by many dischargers, and which are easy to calculate or monitor or for which a comon denominator exists (BOD, COD), can more easily be subjected to emission charges or taxes than pollutants that occur in great variety and small amounts (heavy metals, toxic substances).   For the latter, product charges or taxes could be considered.   Because of the coimplexity of the matter a multi-phase approach is necessary, starting with those pollutants that are easiest to handle and lead to substantial improvements.

31.   The main target groups for economic instruments in the field of water quality policy are industry (chemical, metal, food, pulp and paper, mining, etc), agriculture, and households.

32.   With regard to industry, emission (effluent) charges or taxes could be applied where 1) industry can effectively reduce emissions in response to the charge or taxe; 2) technical innovation is likely to be encouraged and 3) when the level of emissions can reasonably be monitored.

33.   Agricultural pollution from point sources (such as intensive animal husbandry units) can often be controlled by regulatory means, complemented, where effective, by economic instruments in the form of effluent charges or taxes.   Many agricultural problems arise from diffuse application of pesticides, fertilizers, etc.   Charges based on an evaluation of emissions or product charges or taxes on certain inputs could be applied.   The effectiveness of these instruments needs careful evaluation in the overall context of agricultural policy.

Air Pollution

34. In the field of air pollution control, emission charges or taxes may be considered as a complement or a substitute to regulation. For administrative reasons (in particular, monitoring of emissions), emission charges or taxes are more easily applicable to large volume pollutants and large stationary sources.

35. As energy production and use is a major cause of air pollution, energy pricing should take environmental factors into account; this can be done by applying product charges or taxes, in particular charges on fuels in the form of a surcharge on or a variation of the excise duties on fossil fuels. Product charges or taxes can be used as a proxy for emission charges or taxes, for instance when pollution is diffuse, when there are many, small (mobile) sources. There is a strong tradition, especially in the transport sector, for taxation of mobile sources, and these should be adapted in line with environmental objectives.

36. Creating price differentiation between traditional products and cleaner substitutes can be done by a combination of surcharges and discounts on the price of such products in a broadly revenue-neutral way.

37. Marketable permits can be considered in order to create market conditions for new and modified installations and regarding air pollution characteristics of some products (e.g. cars). Producers could be allowed to trade credits by exceeding standards or meeting them earlier than required, providing that equal or better environmental conditions are achieved.

38. Deposit-refund systems can be applied to products that contain potentially polluting substances in closed circuits (e.g. refrigerators and air conditioners containing CFC's). After return, such products can be properly scrapped, or recycled.

39. In the case of air pollution, the main target groups for applying economic instruments are industry, energy and transport. For industry, the same constraints applicable to water pollution (paragraph 31) should be taken into account. For the energy sector, particular attention should be paid to proper integration of energy and environmental policies through appropriate pricing of energy resources.

40. Integration of transport and environmental policies is also of particular relevance. Not only should transport pricing and taxation take into account environmental factors,

but also specific economic instruments could be introduced, such as pricing/taxation of fuels reflecting, as far as possible, the ultimate environmental damage caused. Motor-vehicles could also be subjected to environmental charges or taxes. Congestion charges or taxes, primarily designed to alleviate traffic problems, could contribute to reducing air pollution. Finally, charging for the use of transport infrastructures (road pricing and other tolls) should also integrate environmental concerns, when appropriate.

Waste Management

41.   Financing (user) charges should aim at a proper collection, processing and storage of waste or at the clean up of old hazardous waste sites. Incentive charges or taxes can have multiple purposes which should be recognized when designed. A first purpose might be to minimize (voluminous and/or toxic) waste generation in production and consumption processes. A second purpose might be to discourage production and consumption of (voluminous and/or toxic) waste-intensive products and to promote more "friendly" substitutes. Thirdly, economic instruments can be introduced to promote recycling which saves depletable resources, including space for waste dumping.

42.   Emission (disposal) charges or taxes should be based either on the volume and/or on the toxicity (or other harmful characteristics) of waste elements. In the latter case, waste containing many substances will cause calculation and monitoring problems. Because of possible evasion, emission charges or taxes can only be applied if it is easy to control dischargers. In most cases, user charges, i.e. payment for waste collection and the use of waste disposal facilities, can be applied.

43.   Product charges or taxes can be considered in the case of products that will generate waste in the production or consumption phases (e.g. plastic bags). They act as proxies in those cases where a direct charging for waste is not effective or efficient. Materials which cannot be recycled or re-used could be subjected to charges or taxes.

44.   In the cases where a return of used products to collection or storage sites is important, a deposit-refund system can be considered. This is desirable when such products can be re- used or recycled (bottles, crates) or when such products contain potentially polluting substances (batteries, cars). A product subject to a deposit-refund system should exist in large quantity and the necessary collection system should be manageable.

45. Main target groups for economic instruments in waste management are industry, agriculture, households and the waste handling sector, be it public or private. Industry may be subject to economic instruments, either because they produce products that will create waste problems when used or disposed of, or generate voluminous or toxic wastes. Agricultural waste such as animal manure could also be charged for.

Noise

46. Economic instruments can be used to reinforce direct regulation, improve enforcement of existing measures and speed up compliance with more stringent noise standards. Economic instruments can also improve the integration between different policy fields, in particular between transport policy and noise abatement policy. Economic instruments (charges) are also able to raise revenues for financing specific noise abatement measures, such as the insulation of houses, or the construction of noise barriers.

47. Charges or taxes on noise sources can be considered regarding aircraft noise, road traffic noise and industrial noise sources. Aircraft noise charges or taxes can be applied on landing fees according to noise characteristics of the aircraft and associated with physical regulations (ICAO noise approval certificates). Charges or taxes could also be applied to passenger cars and lorries, based on their acoustic characteristics as measured under internationally agreed procedures (e.g. ISO). Emission charges or taxes are also applicable to (stationary) industrial noise sources.

48. Product charges or taxes could be used with respect to appliances. Differentiation of taxes is conceivable with regard to noisy products and low-noise-alternatives.

49. Other economic instruments which are considered with respect to other traffic problems, such as road pricing and charging according to the costs of car use, could also work in relation to noise. Noise charges or taxes could also be part of an integrated charging system on motor-vehicles, comprising pollution and other possible characteristics of vehicles.

50. The main target groups for the application of economic instruments to noise are transport, owners of domestic appliances and industry. Regarding transport, manufacturers and users of passenger cars and lorries, airports and railways should be considered. Regarding industry, a variety of sectors are involved; among these are the construction sector and many large manufacturers.

Applying Economic Instruments to International and Global Environmental Problems

51.   Economic instruments can be considered for tackling international and global environmental problems, such as acid rain, global warming and stratospheric ozone depletion, in the most cost-effective manner.

52.   Carbon dioxide is the main factor causing global warming, but emissions cannot be removed by any end-of-pipe treatment currently available. However, since emissions are proportional to the carbon content of the fuels being burned, a charge or tax on carbon would be identical to an emission charge or taxe on carbon dioxide. The charge or taxe on carbon could be translated into a product charge or taxe on fossil fuels given information about the carbon content of these fuels. Likewise, the tax system may be adapted, for example through a taxation of the sulphur content of fuels. General measures such as energy taxes or charges should, in conformity with other policy objectives, encourage increased energy efficiency, thereby lowering related environmental impacts.

53.   Marketable permits can also be considered. If the goal is to hold emissions constant, some existing emission sources could be allowed to increase emissions, and new sources could be allowed to emit, provided that they can get some other source to reduce emissions by at least an equivalent amount. Alternatively, increases in emissions could be offset by investments which increase the environment's ability to absorb the emissions (in the case of carbon dioxide).

54.   Target groups vary from problem to problem. For instance, a limited umber of firms produce CFCs and these could be subjected to charges or marketable permits. For practical reasons, marketable permits would have to apply to producers and importers only. Large emission sources of carbon dioxide like electricity producers could be allocated marketable permits or be made subject to carbon charges or taxes. Small sources like households could also be subject to a carbon charge or taxe (for example, on gasoline and home heating fuels).

130

MAIN SALES OUTLETS OF OECD PUBLICATIONS
PRINCIPAUX POINTS DE VENTE DES PUBLICATIONS DE L'OCDE

ARGENTINA – ARGENTINE
Carlos Hirsch S.R.L.
Galería Güemes, Florida 165, 4° Piso
1333 Buenos Aires Tel. (1) 331.1787 y 331.2391
Telefax: (1) 331.1787

AUSTRALIA – AUSTRALIE
D.A. Book (Aust.) Pty. Ltd.
648 Whitehorse Road, P.O.B 163
Mitcham, Victoria 3132 Tel. (03) 873.4411
Telefax: (03) 873.5679

AUSTRIA – AUTRICHE
Gerold & Co.
Graben 31
Wien I Tel. (0222) 533.50.14

BELGIUM – BELGIQUE
Jean De Lannoy
Avenue du Roi 202
B-1060 Bruxelles Tel. (02) 538.51.69/538.08.41
Telefax: (02) 538.08.41

CANADA
Renouf Publishing Company Ltd.
1294 Algoma Road
Ottawa, ON K1B 3W8 Tel. (613) 741.4333
Telefax: (613) 741.5439
Stores:
61 Sparks Street
Ottawa, ON K1P 5R1 Tel. (613) 238.8985
211 Yonge Street
Toronto, ON M5B 1M4 Tel. (416) 363.3171
Les Éditions La Liberté Inc.
3020 Chemin Sainte-Foy
Sainte-Foy, PQ G1X 3V6 Tel. (418) 658.3763
Telefax: (418) 658.3763

Federal Publications
165 University Avenue
Toronto, ON M5H 3B8 Tel. (416) 581.1552
Telefax: (416) 581.1743

CHINA – CHINE
China National Publications Import
Export Corporation (CNPIEC)
16 Gongti E. Road, Chaoyang District
P.O. Box 88 or 50
Beijing 100704 PR Tel. (01) 506.6688
Telefax: (01) 506.3101

DENMARK – DANEMARK
Munksgaard Export and Subscription Service
35, Nørre Søgade, P.O. Box 2148
DK-1016 København K Tel. (33) 12.85.70
Tel. (33) 12.93.87

FINLAND – FINLANDE
Akateeminen Kirjakauppa
Keskuskatu 1, P.O. Box 128
00100 Helsinki Tel. (358 0) 12141
Telefax: (358 0) 121.4441

FRANCE
OECD/OCDE
Mail Orders/Commandes par correspondance:
2, rue André-Pascal
75775 Paris Cedex 16 Tel. (33-1) 45.24.82.00
Telefax: (33-1) 45.24.85.00 or (33-1) 45.24.81.76
Telex: 640048 OCDE

OECD Bookshop/Librairie de l'OCDE :
33, rue Octave-Feuillet
75016 Paris Tel. (33-1) 45.24.81.67
(33-1) 45.24.81.81

Documentation Française
29, quai Voltaire
75007 Paris Tel. 40.15.70.00

Gibert Jeune (Droit-Économie)
6, place Saint-Michel
75006 Paris Tel. 43.25.91.19

Librairie du Commerce International
10, avenue d'Iéna
75016 Paris Tel. 40.73.34.60
Librairie Dunod
Université Paris-Dauphine
Place du Maréchal de Lattre de Tassigny
75016 Paris Tel. 47.27.18.56
Librairie Lavoisier
11, rue Lavoisier
75008 Paris Tel. 42.65.39.95
Librairie L.G.D.J. - Montchrestien
20, rue Soufflot
75005 Paris Tel. 46.33.89.85
Librairie des Sciences Politiques
30, rue Saint-Guillaume
75007 Paris Tel. 45.48.36.02
P.U.F.
49, boulevard Saint-Michel
75005 Paris Tel. 43.25.83.40
Librairie de l'Université
12a, rue Nazareth
13100 Aix-en-Provence Tel. (16) 42.26.18.08
Documentation Française
165, rue Garibaldi
69003 Lyon Tel. (16) 78.63.32.23
Librairie Decitre
29, place Bellecour
69002 Lyon Tel. (16) 72.40.54.54

GERMANY – ALLEMAGNE
OECD Publications and Information Centre
Schedestrasse 7
D-W 5300 Bonn 1 Tel. (0228) 21.60.45
Telefax: (0228) 26.11.04

GREECE – GRÈCE
Librairie Kauffmann
Mavrokordatou 9
106 78 Athens Tel. 322.21.60
Telefax: 363.39.67

HONG-KONG
Swindon Book Co. Ltd.
13–15 Lock Road
Kowloon, Hong Kong Tel. 366.80.31
Telefax: 739.49.75

ICELAND – ISLANDE
Mál Mog Menning
Laugavegi 18, Pósthólf 392
121 Reykjavik Tel. 162.35.23

INDIA – INDE
Oxford Book and Stationery Co.
Scindia House
New Delhi 110001 Tel.(11) 331.5896/5308
Telefax: (11) 332.5993
17 Park Street
Calcutta 700016 Tel. 240832

INDONESIA – INDONÉSIE
Pdii-Lipi
P.O. Box 269/JKSMG/88
Jakarta 12790 Tel. 583467
Telex: 62 875

IRELAND – IRLANDE
TDC Publishers – Library Suppliers
12 North Frederick Street
Dublin 1 Tel. 74.48.35/74.96.77
Telefax: 74.84.16

ISRAEL
Electronic Publications only
Publications électroniques seulement
Sophist Systems Ltd.
71 Allenby Street
Tel-Aviv 65134 Tel. 3-29.00.21
Telefax: 3-29.92.39

ITALY – ITALIE
Libreria Commissionaria Sansoni
Via Duca di Calabria 1/1
50125 Firenze Tel. (055) 64.54.15
Telefax: (055) 64.12.57
Via Bartolini 29
20155 Milano Tel. (02) 36.50.83
Editrice e Libreria Herder
Piazza Montecitorio 120
00186 Roma Tel. 679.46.28
Telefax: 678.47.51
Libreria Hoepli
Via Hoepli 5
20121 Milano Tel. (02) 86.54.46
Telefax: (02) 805.28.86
Libreria Scientifica
Dott. Lucio de Biasio 'Aeiou'
Via Coronelli, 6
20146 Milano Tel. (02) 48.95.45.52
Telefax: (02) 48.95.45.48

JAPAN – JAPON
OECD Publications and Information Centre
Landic Akasaka Building
2-3-4 Akasaka, Minato-ku
Tokyo 107 Tel. (81.3) 3586.2016
Telefax: (81.3) 3584.7929

KOREA – CORÉE
Kyobo Book Centre Co. Ltd.
P.O. Box 1658, Kwang Hwa Moon
Seoul Tel. 730.78.91
Telefax: 735.00.30

MALAYSIA – MALAISIE
Co-operative Bookshop Ltd.
University of Malaya
P.O. Box 1127, Jalan Pantai Baru
59700 Kuala Lumpur
Malaysia Tel. 756.5000/756.5425
Telefax: 757.3661

NETHERLANDS – PAYS-BAS
SDU Uitgeverij
Christoffel Plantijnstraat 2
Postbus 20014
2500 EA's-Gravenhage Tel. (070 3) 78.99.11
Voor bestellingen: Tel. (070 3) 78.98.80
Telefax: (070 3) 47.63.51

NEW ZEALAND
NOUVELLE-ZÉLANDE
Legislation Services
P.O. Box 12418
Thorndon, Wellington Tel. (04) 496.5652
Telefax: (04) 496.5698

NORWAY – NORVÈGE
Narvesen Info Center – NIC
Bertrand Narvesens vei 2
P.O. Box 6125 Etterstad
0602 Oslo 6 Tel. (02) 57.33.00
Telefax: (02) 68.19.01

PAKISTAN
Mirza Book Agency
65 Shahrah Quaid-E-Azam
Lahore 3 Tel. 66.839
Telex: 44886 UBL PK. Attn: MIRZA BK

PORTUGAL
Livraria Portugal
Rua do Carmo 70-74
Apart. 2681
1117 Lisboa Codex Tel.: (01) 347.49.82/3/4/5
Telefax: (01) 347.02.64

SINGAPORE – SINGAPOUR
Information Publications Pte. Ltd.
41, Kallang Pudding, No. 04-03
Singapore 1334   Tel. 741.5166
                                 Telefax: 742.9356

SPAIN – ESPAGNE
Mundi-Prensa Libros S.A.
Castelló 37, Apartado 1223
Madrid 28001   Tel. (91) 431.33.99
                                 Telefax: (91) 575.39.98
Libreria Internacional AEDOS
Consejo de Ciento 391
08009 – Barcelona   Tel. (93) 488.34.92
                                 Telefax: (93) 487.76.59
Llibreria de la Generalitat
Palau Moja
Rambla dels Estudis, 118
08002 – Barcelona
          (Subscripcions) Tel. (93) 318.80.12
          (Publicacions) Tel. (93) 302.67.23
                         Telefax: (93) 412.18.54

SRI LANKA
Centre for Policy Research
c/o Colombo Agencies Ltd.
No. 300-304, Galle Road
Colombo 3   Tel. (1) 574240, 573551-2
                 Telefax: (1) 575394, 510711

SWEDEN – SUÈDE
Fritzes Fackboksföretaget
Box 16356
Regeringsgatan 12
103 27 Stockholm   Tel. (08) 23.89.00
                                 Telefax: (08) 20.50.21
Subscription Agency-Agence d'abonnements
Wennergren-Williams AB
Nordenflychtsvägen 74
Box 30004
104 25 Stockholm   Tel. (08) 13.67.00
                                 Telefax: (08) 618.62.36

SWITZERLAND – SUISSE
Maditec S.A. (Books and Periodicals - Livres
et périodiques)
Chemin des Palettes 4
1020 Renens/Lausanne   Tel. (021) 635.08.65
                                 Telefax: (021) 635.07.80

Librairie Payot
Service des Publications Internationales
Case postale 3212
1002 Lausanne   Tel. (021) 341.33.48
                                 Telefax: (021) 341.33.45

Librairie Unilivres
6, rue de Candolle
1205 Genève   Tel. (022) 320.26.23
                                 Telefax: (022) 329.73.18

Subscription Agency - Agence d'abonnement
Naville S.A.
38 avenue Vibert
1227 Carouge   Tél.: (022) 308.05.56/57
                                 Telefax: (022) 308.05.88

See also – Voir aussi :
OECD Publications and Information Centre
Schedestrasse 7
D-W 5300 Bonn 1 (Germany)
                                 Tel. (49.228) 21.60.45
                                 Telefax: (49.228) 26.11.04

TAIWAN – FORMOSE
Good Faith Worldwide Int'l. Co. Ltd.
9th Floor, No. 118, Sec. 2
Chung Hsiao E. Road
Taipei   Tel. (02) 391.7396/391.7397
                                 Telefax: (02) 394.9176

THAILAND – THAÏLANDE
Suksit Siam Co. Ltd.
113, 115 Fuang Nakhon Rd.
Opp. Wat Rajbopith
Bangkok 10200   Tel. (662) 251.1630
                                 Telefax: (662) 236.7783

TURKEY – TURQUIE
Kültur Yayinlari Is-Türk Ltd. Sti.
Atatürk Bulvari No. 191/Kat. 13
Kavaklidere/Ankara   Tel. 428.11.40 Ext. 2458
Dolmabahce Cad. No. 29
Besiktas/Istanbul   Tel. 160.71.88
                                 Telex: 43482B

UNITED KINGDOM – ROYAUME-UNI
HMSO
Gen. enquiries   Tel. (071) 873 0011
Postal orders only:
P.O. Box 276, London SW8 5DT
Personal Callers HMSO Bookshop
49 High Holborn, London WC1V 6HB
                                 Telefax: (071) 873 8200
Branches at: Belfast, Birmingham, Bristol, Edin-
burgh, Manchester

UNITED STATES – ÉTATS-UNIS
OECD Publications and Information Centre
2001 L Street N.W., Suite 700
Washington, D.C. 20036-4910 Tel. (202) 785.6323
                                 Telefax: (202) 785.0350

VENEZUELA
Libreria del Este
Avda F. Miranda 52, Aptdo. 60337
Edificio Galipán
Caracas 106   Tel. 951.1705/951.2307/951.1297
                 Telegram: Libreste Caracas

Subscription to OECD periodicals may also be
placed through main subscription agencies.

Les abonnements aux publications périodiques de
l'OCDE peuvent être souscrits auprès des
principales agences d'abonnement.

Orders and inquiries from countries where Distributors have not yet been appointed should be sent to:
OECD Publications Service, 2 rue André-Pascal,
75775 Paris Cedex 16, France.

Les commandes provenant de pays où l'OCDE n'a
pas encore désigné de distributeur devraient être
adressées à : OCDE, Service des Publications,
2, rue André-Pascal, 75775 Paris Cedex 16, France.

                                                  10-1992

OECD PUBLICATIONS, 2 rue André-Pascal, 75775 PARIS CEDEX 16
PRINTED IN FRANCE
(97 91 03 1) ISBN 92-64-13568-5 - No. 45565 1991